Every Drop of Water

and

Every Grain of Salt

on the

Way to Authentic Happiness

Dr. Armando S. Garcia

To

The love of my life,

my wife Sandra,

and

to the joys of my life,

my children Arthur and Samantha

Table of Contents

Preface ix

Introduction xiii

I

The Salt

On the Subjective Manifestation of Consciousness 1

The Self 11

The Truth About Suffering 16

Desiderata 25

The Emotional Me 31

Fear of Freedom 37

The Others 42

The Problem with Happiness 47

II

The Water

The Personal Universe 55

Being a Good Person 63

Being with Others 71

Being Not-self 78

Being out of Time 85

Being and *That* 90

Letting Go 93

Right Mindfulness 103

Right Parenting 108

III

Being

Authentic Happiness 117

Nothing Meditation 122

Enlightenment and Unbinding 130

Bibliography 137

Preface

During my past 24 years as a pediatrician, I have had the privilege and pleasure of observing the blossoming of countless young minds, many from birth to adolescence. Throughout this time, I have often been impressed and delighted to witness the remarkable urge for autonomy and the innate self-confidence exhibited by young children. Even the young toddler, despite an almost total dependence on the parent, already demonstrates an awareness of self as different from the world and an exuberance for independence. What has impressed me the most, however, and served as an inspiration for this book, is the joyfulness and contentment which is characteristic of most young children, even in the face of significant suffering. These expressions, of innate joyfulness, boldness, and a penchant for independence, were the beacons which guided me to recognize the inherent meaningfulness and plentitude of the unencumbered consciousness.

What I observe in my interaction with even a one-month old infant is a completely developed consciousness which is learning to use its body. That is, the body of an infant is immature, the consciousness is not, it is completely there. The infant is not like a little organic robot fleshed out of the genes of the parents, with a con-sciousness generated by the electro-chemical reactions of a devel-oping brain. Rather, the behavior of the infant already reflects a being-there, a presence, a consciousness already consummated, which is not like anything else in the physical world, a truly won-drous and mysterious thing. This pure, radiant awareness is what resonates deeply with the parents, generating incomparable joy. It is what I designate as essential Being.

Unfortunately, our pure and transparent awareness dulls and darkens as it becomes involved with the world. This is what I have also witnessed: the constriction of the joyfulness, the boldness, and natural assertiveness of the young mind as it grows into the frus-trated and stressed adolescent. As children, most of us experience the world with a candid and uncomplicated mind, with an uncon-ditioned openness to life and others, and with a pleasure in simply existing. Yet, as we grow older and are confronted with the chal-lenges and misfortunes of life, this simple way of being is increas-ingly replaced with cluttered memories, concerns, and fears; our aged minds frequently suffering from neurosis and obsessions. This clouding and blunting of the mind are a natural consequence of our development as free individuals, but it is something which we are compelled to transcend.

Indeed, human existence has always been and will always be a struggle: for food, for shelter, for safety, to reproduce, to find hap-piness, to find meaning. As a physician, I have been privileged to the miracles of the human body, and to its relentless fight against infections and disease. But what I find is the greatest hindrance to lasting happiness is our own self-consciousness. It is our ignorance of what constitutes our true essence which is the source of our greatest suffering and our worst miseries. It is the confused mind which is the begetter of wars, homicide, suicide, abuse, and most of our daily discontent. It is to this extent that I wrote this book: to bring to awareness the origin of our unhappiness and to point the way to true happiness.

This book shows the way back to the unencumbered mind of the child. It reveals how our unawareness of our existential Nothingness conditions a grasping of the world as Self, causing unnecessary stress and suffering; and how, by finding our centeredness in Being, we regain our peace of mind and authentic happiness.

While there are many books these days with instructions on how to develop the positive mental habits that lead to a happier attitude, they all miss a most important point: that our desire for happiness is about much more than just wanting to feel happy. This book reveals why our search for happiness is in effect the quest for our true self.

The concept of *being* dates back to the ancient Greek philosophers in their analysis of existence, and was made popular in more recent times by the philosopher Martin Heidegger in his examination of Being—capitalized to indicate human being—as that being which is aware of the existence of other beings and conscious of its own existence. Other authors have used Being to signify a universal consciousness, akin to a god. My use of Being here, however, is in its participle verb form, specifically referring to an *individual experience of existing*: the experience of what it is to exist.

In part because of our ability to become habituated to almost any situation—which has allowed humanity to thrive in the most inhospitable of circumstances—and in part because our conscious point of view is an absolute subjectivity, that we humans appear to suffer from a natural insensitivity to what is closest to us. As what could be called the Law of Apperceptive Opacity, we find that the closer something is to our point of view the more blurred it becomes to our apperception, such that, as we move backward from town, to neighborhood, to street, family, the body, and the self, our objective judgments become increasingly obscured, so that we are almost entirely blind to what is most intrinsically us: our very Being.

We have become so rational in modern times, that we have lost sight of what it means to exist, to be. Yet, it is Being which gives meaning to our existence and which conditions the moral structure of our relationships. As such, it is at once the most obvious, the most profound, and the most obscure thing.

Introduction

Everyone wants to be happy. Our expectation of happiness is the prime motivation for almost everything we do or avoid doing. It would seem then that figuring out what happiness is, and how to get it, should be the easiest and most natural thing to do. However, psychologists and philosophers have wrestled with this question for centuries without finding a definitive answer. The problem is that our perception of happiness depends on the nature of our consciousness, and human consciousness is not like anything else in the world: it is a Nothingness. Our pursuit of happiness is in effect a quest for our True Self—not an easy task.

As it turns out, most of us typically end up chasing the wrong kind of happiness: what we are really after is satisfaction. We create a desire, and if it works out then we are pleased, satisfied—and we call it happiness, and if it doesn't then we are frustrated, then angry or depressed. As a result, we end up spending a lot of time and money running after elusive gratifications and running away from incomprehensible suffering. We will see how desire is the crux of our unhappiness, and how contentment is, in fact, our fundamental state of mind.

The World Happiness Report is a yearly survey published by the United Nations which ranks about 150 countries according to social, psychological, and economic parameters. Since its first report in 2012, the U.S. has been steadily dropping in rank in the index of happiness, down to 18 on the 2018 report, despite economic growth and decreased unemployment in the past few years. Furthermore, although 80% of adults have a social media account and about 95% of young adults and teens use social media regularly, a survey done by the Cigna insurance company of nearly 20,000 adults across the country, found that 54% reported feeling lonely and isolated. The National Mental Health Institute reports about 15% of the U.S. population experiencing significant depression yearly. Recent studies also show that more than half of U.S. workers are unhappy with their employment. It seems that, despite our great national wealth, many in the U.S. are unhappy.

Now, wealth can satisfy a lot of desires, but as many can attest, this is a bottomless pit. You can get excited to buy the nicest purse, designer shoes and jewelry, go on a dream vacation, have a home on the beach with a boat, but after some time, everything has lost its novelty, and you are wishing for more. It is disheartening that we study and work hard to achieve our dreams, putting up with adversity and abuse, giving up personal freedom and the attention to family, and at the end of the day our hard-earned wealth and success, and our purchases, leave us unfulfilled—our family and health sometimes suffering the consequences of our neglect. What is wrong? What's missing? And if wealth, education, and success cannot guarantee lasting happiness, then what does?

For one thing, it is a matter of hygiene. These days it seems most everyone is overeating and then trying to lose weight with the latest fashionable diet, enthusiastically joining cutting-edge exercise programs, eagerly consuming the newest app or electronic gimmick, and watching the latest movie or sitcom, while the attention to the internal life, our psychological hygiene, is severely lacking or non-existent. While many of us are working hard to look good in the mirror, our mental life is full of mental waste. If you pay careful attention to your thoughts for even a few minutes, if you are like most people, you will notice that most of what you think about is of little importance or benefit, and even more, only serves to incite your emotions, which then cause unnecessary stress. A great part of our thinking involves ruminations over things we have said, or wish we hadn't said or done, about unreasonable fears, about fantasies of the future, or just daydreaming, often running for long periods with self-directed dialog, which ultimately leave the mind stressed and drained; overtime, the clutter of negative and stressful thoughts weighing the mind down with regrets, resentments, prejudices, sadness, or depression.

This book shows the way to a healthy, clean, and peaceful mind. You will understand why our ignorance of the true nature of our consciousness and our careless mental habits, gradually lead to significant psychological burdens. You will learn how to develop the wisdom and the wholesome attitudes which bring about lasting happiness.

It is excellent if you take good care of yourself by exercising regularly and eating healthy—you will probably live a long time. But of what good is a long, healthy, unhappy life. If you can't live your life with contentment, peace of mind, and a feeling of personal fulfillment, then what is the sense of it all?

Maybe you've tried one, or many, of the many self-help books out on the market these days, or participate in an established, or newer, religious institution in hopes of finding a deeper connection to life; but if you cannot spend a quiet afternoon, without doing anything, without feeling restless or anxious, then something fundamental is missing.

The good news is that it doesn't have to be one thing or the other. We don't have to give up the fruits of our hard-earned success, we don't have to change our religion, become a hermit, sit in a lotus position, or give up sex, to realize authentic happiness; but we do need to give some time and attention to our mind—it does take some effort to clean up the mess. Here, however, I am not talking about "mindfulness" only. Lately, it seems that there is a mindfulness application for almost everything—and it is good, but it is not enough. By itself mindfulness, or "being in the present moment," does not detox the mind; it only helps you see what the problem is.

This is not a pop psychology "don't worry, be happy" one-quick-read book. It is also not a book filled with anecdotes for your entertainment. The serious questions in life, questions about true happiness, meaningfulness, free will, morality, and self-identity, are founded on the very mystery of our humanity and are therefore not easy to see or to face. Most of us sidestep these imperatives until the bottom falls out of our life plan, or until the Grim Reaper is tapping on the shoulder. As it is, there are no quick fixes to removing years and years of bad mental habits. Nevertheless, even with a casual understanding of the principles presented here, you will achieve significant contentment and peacefulness of mind; with a thorough study and dedicated practice, an entirely new and wonderful perspective on life can open up for you.

The fact that you have picked up this book is already an indication that you are seeing past the delusion and fantasies of our hyper-digital world: you are, like Neo from *The Matrix*, seeing a glitch in the system. The technological advances we witness today are near miraculous; with so many means of "connecting," the world has become a much smaller—not better—place. But while our resources for information and communication are ever expanding, what is mostly communicated is entertainment. Between texting, YouTube, Facebook, Twitter, and personal emails there is little time to watch your favorite television shows and even less to talk with the kids, spouse, or significant other. Not that there is anything wrong with entertainment, but when it takes up most of your day-life, it becomes escapism. And what are we escaping from? We are running away from the very source of our anxieties and stress: The Nothingness.

Now, when children are bad, they get a timeout, and when prisoners are really bad, they are put into solitary confinement; it appears that us humans have a natural aversion to solitude—like cats to water. For one thing, when the mind is not busy attending to something, then all kinds of uncomfortable memories, exaggerated preoccupations, and unfounded fears tend come forth like ghosts that have been waiting for the night; then we reject, suppress, elaborate, or rationalize these consuming thoughts in an effort to get them to go away. The more negative your life has been, the more powerful, threatening, and numerous these phantoms; some people turning to drugs or alcohol to numb the mind, to find some rest. The problem with our solitude, as we will discuss, has all to do with the nature of our consciousness as a Nothingness, and it is something that we will need to face to find peace of mind—as we cannot run away from our mental specters any more than we can run away from our shadow.

In conclusion, what we are lacking in this busy age of technology is just some peace and quiet to come to terms with our Self and our Nothingness. We need to make some time to explore our inner virtual world, our mind, because this fast-paced world appears to be getting us nowhere. We must face our existential emptiness, to discover who we truly are, what this life is ultimately about, and what begets authentic happiness. This book will help you make the best of your quiet time.

We will begin our journey of Self-discovery by analyzing the fundamental problem with our self-identity: *The Self who we are not.* We will evaluate how this Self is our necessary means of becoming, but not of Being, and how it foments our suffering and eclipses our freedom. We will examine the enigmatic truth about suffering, which just like the Self, is indispensable for our healthy development as individuals. We will learn that our fundamental reaction to the world is one of fear: fear of others, fear of being free, and fear of non-being. We will explore how our ignorance as to the nature of the Self conditions our state of mind, our relationships, and our perception of happiness. Throughout our lifetime the Self grows increasingly complex and heavy with resentments, guilt, jealousies, and unresolved conflicts; it becomes saturated with obstinate mental habits and despondent with the aging body; not infrequently succumbing to anxiety, neurosis, or depression. It is disheartening that so many of us carry these afflictions into old age not knowing how to put them down. And unfortunately, letting go is not as simple as just letting go.

Everything discussed here you will be able to verify for yourself as to its accuracy and veracity by simply observing your own mind, and because you have a front row seat to your own psyche, you can become your own best psychologist.

Throughout, we will employ a glass of saltwater as a model for our comprehensive psychological constitution—our mental baggage. Everything we do, everything we intend, or even think, changes us to some extent. Just like one grain of salt in a glass of water is imperceptible, and many grains make water unpalatable, and a still greater amount crystalizes, so do our moral transgressions gradually accumulate, slowly and imperceptibly corrupting us, eventually irrevocably. In the first section, "The Salt," we shall explore the aspects of our existence which produce salt: which disrupt the natural peacefulness of the mind, causing stress, and conditioning our suffering. Water conforms, it is naturally nonresistant, at rest it becomes transparent and serene. Our good intentions, good actions, and good mental habits are as water: washing out and diluting the impurities of the mind, and in large quantities bringing forth wisdom and transcendence. In the second section, "The Water," we will explore the ways we can add more water to the salt in our glass.

Now, the conditions of our existence are such that we are already born with some salt in the glass; this is a result of our physical existence in the flesh and on this earth, of our evolutionary development, our social and cultural environment, and our family history. Another condition, or complication, is that due to the nature of our consciousness, for the most part, it is very difficult to get rid of the salt; it is much easier to add water. The amount of salt and water in our psychological glass determines our mental state, and therefore, our peace of mind and subsequent happiness, and as we will see, we are unconditionally free to add as much water or salt as we like. This book is about the many ways by which we create the salt in our lives, and how we can learn to add more water to what we have. Unfortunately, most of us don't foresee the consequences of too much salt or too little water until it is too late, as it depends on every grain of salt and every drop of water along the way.

I

The Salt

On the Subjective Manifestation of Consciousness

Reclined on the seat of a 747-jumbo jet—windows are closed for the night—relaxing in the dimly lit cabin, I am aware of the softness of the cushioned seat, of a slight rocking of the plane now and then, of the dull humming of the engines; what I am not aware of is that my body is traveling at 550 mph. This is because I am moving at the same speed as the plane, and I don't have a frame of reference to compare with. However, when I am looking at a plane taking off from a runway, I can easily observe how fast it is moving. Now at this point you are probably thinking "so what," but this is very important, because it illustrates the difficult problem posed by our consciousness in the perception of who we are.

Cogito ergo sum, "I think; therefore, I am," was declared by the philosopher Rene Descartes back in 1637 in his treatise regarding the nature of knowledge. Everything that I know can be doubted, he stated, except for the fact that I think—and ergo fomenting the obsession of western culture with thinking ever since. As it is with most people, if I were to ask "who are you," I would be given a name, age, body characteristics, occupation, family or ethnic history, etc., that is, a conceptual description of your self-perception.

In other words, we create a self-identity out of ideas that we have about who we are: about what we like and dislike, our beliefs, from our memories since childhood, from our impressions of how we are perceived, and projections of who we want to be; this we will call the Self. The Self is simply made of thoughts. Now, consider that when you are thinking, what you perceive are a series of thoughts which come and go, and there is *you*, as the observer of the thoughts, tying them together—like watching cars passing by. As in the illustration of the airplane, if the thinker were *each thought* then the thinker would be an unconsciousness: you would not be aware that you are thinking. Or there would be an absurd regression of a thought watching other thoughts, then another thought watching other thoughts, ad infinitum. *That is, awareness cannot be part of the series of things and be outside watching the series at the same time.* Therefore, there must be a consciousness which is aware of the thoughts, which sits outside of the thoughts. This is what the existential philosophers call the non-reflective (or sometimes the pre-reflective) consciousness; the reflective consciousness being the thinking. It is this non-reflective consciousness, which is the basis of all conscious experience, which *knows* before we think, before we reflect. However, it is not an unconsciousness. Since the Age of Reason, we have become so rational, so dependent on linguistic thinking, that the origin of *knowing* has faded to a background, seeming an unconsciousness from the perspective of reflection. Notwithstanding, once you identify this all-encompassing awareness, it becomes remarkably obvious that the *One who thinks* is not the thoughts.

Thinking is something that human consciousness does, not what it is. Anyone who looks into the eyes of even a very young infant has no doubts that there is a *knowing* there, an awareness. Already at 6 months of age an infant is investigating and interacting with his or her world, and at one year he/she demonstrate preferences and wants, thus demonstrating awareness and understanding even though words do not significantly develop until 18 months of age. In fact, most of the "thinking" we do is non-verbal. I look at my watch and suddenly become aware I am late for work, then a second later I verbalize in my head "Oh no, I'm late for work." I don't mentally verbalize when putting on pants, or buttoning my shirt, or combing, but I may very well comment to myself on the color or style that would be best to wear. When I am shaving or brushing my teeth, I may be thinking about something entirely un-related, like the conversation I had with my wife the night before. I am not shaving subconsciously, I am just not using my words for that awareness, but I do think with words when I am recalling a conversation. Almost everything we do, from walking, eating, and observing everything around us, we do without verbal reflection. As a young man I remember driving from Boston to New York without being aware of it, the entire time lost in thoughts, yet obey-ing the speed limits and traffic signs without really thinking about it. I was not driving subconsciously; I was just not reflecting on it.

While thinking, listening, concentrating, and focusing require mental en-ergy, being conscious requires no energy expenditure, no effort at all: it is a spontaneous clear unitary awareness which underlies all reflective activity.

The non-reflective consciousness is the basis of all apprehen-sion of the world. Although it appears that we have a consciousness which is inside the body and looking out at a solid world, as if look-ing through a window, in reality it is the world that is *inside* our consciousness. Suppose that no one in the world can see colors, that we can only experience the world in black and white. How could we detect colors? We could examine the different wave-lengths of white light, but they would only appear as different fre-quencies of grey; there would be no red, or green, no blue sky, all our experiments would reveal a grey world.

Philosophers have for a long time known that we can only per-ceive the world through our senses, and that we use this sensory information to synthesize perceptions and ideas; but still, there has always been a philosophical struggle to make contact with a purely objective reality: to know what is really out there. This apprehension of the real world, unmarred by our consciousness of it, becomes especially important concerning the accuracy of scientific investigation and knowledge. To address this problem, a philosopher by the name of Edmund Husserl (b.1859, d.1938) developed a radical technique he called Phenomenological Reduction, were the universe of *existents* is appreciated in its purity of conscious expression by "bracketing off", or transcending, any presumptions and rational understanding of it: by *knowing* what there *is* rather than thinking about it. What Husserl concluded was that all that can be determined to exist for us is just the *phenomenon*, or the appearance of the world as a *conscious impression*; that is, consciousness and the physical world affect each other in the conscious experience of the phenomenon; what is beyond that conscious impression, is out of our perceptual reach. In other words, what he proposed is that the world is in our minds, as conscious impressions, as the phenomenon. Now if the objects of the world are in the mind as conscious impressions, as the phenomenon, then there must be another consciousness which *looks* at these objects of the mind. This consciousness that *looks* at and knows the objects of the mind is the origin of awareness: the non-reflective consciousness, or *the point of view*. What we will call the World (capitalized to indicate all possible conscious perceptions), including not only the physical world, but also thoughts, memories, and emotions, is the *impression* the physical world makes on consciousness.

But if our true essence is non-reflection, then how can we *know* our own existence? And if all possible experience of the World is not who we are, then, how can we know who or what we are? Or, is there then another awareness which is prior to non-reflection?

There cannot be another awareness of the non-reflective awareness because then we are back to an impossible endless regression of aware-nesses. As the existential philosopher Jean Paul Sartre (b.1905, d.1980) explained, the non-reflective consciousness must be conscious of itself in the very process of being conscious of something: It must all at once know itself in the act of knowing something. However, in being a point of view, I am absolutely unable to observe myself, and therefore I am essentially an *absolute subjectivity*.

All this may sound a little convoluted, but it is easier to realize if you sit with your eyes closed in a quiet place and just watch your thoughts as they come and go from your field of awareness—although to do this may take some practice. What you will notice is that thoughts do not linger much, but come and go in the mind, one after the other. It is then, from this vantage point of view, that we can state that the thoughts, feelings, memories, and emotions are not our "true self," because these are the things we are watching appear and disappear. We cannot objectively observe the nature of our own awareness because we are the awareness: *I have no frame of reference to my own consciousness*. However, the nature of consciousness is such that the act of observing reveals the observer, the act of knowing reveals the knower; just like the act of seeing reveals our visual point of view, even though you cannot directly see your eyes seeing.

If you still doubt, then do this experiment. Close the left eye, now with the right finger push gently in on the upper eyelid of the right eye and do this back and forth a few times. What you will have noticed is that you are moving image of the world with your finger, and the reason you can do this is because the world is in the mind: you are a consciousness looking a world *made out of consciousness*. If this were not the case then moving the eye with the finger would appear just as moving the eye as usual, without moving the image, as if looking through a moving window. In a way which is still a mystery for science, the brain creates an image out of sensory information, and the observing consciousness makes it *real,* as a conscious impression. The consciousness-observing and the consciousness-observed cannot be two different consciousness, as then we would again run into an infinite regression of observing consciousnesses (for how would they be connected?): There must be just one consciousness which is affected or impressed upon by the physical world through the nervous system. Consciousness seems to resemble more a floodlight, causing the world to appear out of the darkness, where the source of light originates out of Nothing. Here consciousness is the light emanating from the point of view, but consciousness is also what shines off things, what brings things out of the darkness; the true nature of the objects which shine with the light of consciousness, we can never know.

It is the nature of our consciousness, of our human condition, that we are observers of the World: as a point of view outside of the World. By the World, again, we designate not only the material world but *everything* that we are conscious of, *everything* that we can experience (i.e., the body, the physical world, thoughts, emotions, memories). The fact is that the Self, or ego, which we *think* we are, is just that, a creation of our thinking, just another object of our mind. Throughout our lifetime we create a Self out of the stuff of the World: our body, our education, social status, memories, and everything else we experience. Eventually, we feel we bring it all together as a "personality," with a career, family, possessions, religious affiliation, etc.; a personality which we continuously struggle to preserve against an aggressive world which relentlessly threatens to disintegrate it. This Self, this ego, this person, which we suffer so much to protect, is not who we truly are; it is our creation.

If you attend carefully to your mind, you will find that *everything* which you are able to experience is an *object for your awareness*. We are unable to *directly* observe anything of our subjectivity: This is our Nothingness, our No-thingness. It is this ability of the human consciousness to retract itself beyond the World, into the Nothing, which allows it to be conscious of things. Furthermore, it is the Nothingness that makes it possible for us to be conscious of the

Self as other than things. That is, if our consciousness were made out of any-thing, it would be an un-self-consciousness.

The existentialist philosopher Jean Paul Sartre candidly described human condition as "a being, the nature of which is to be conscious of the nothingness of its being." It is because I am looking at a World which does not belong to me, which is foreign to my essence, since everything which I can experience is not me and is not mine, that I am nothing—a no-thing. This creates an existential *lack,* an emptiness, which we strain to fill with what we see: with the World. We create a Self to fill this essential emptiness, to exist as Something!

This is very important, because it is the strong conviction that we are this artificial Self which is the fundamental cause of our suffering: This is our primordial ignorance. It is what binds us to the world, what destroys our freedom, what creates the salt. And it is the realization of the intrinsic freedom of the mind, as not the Self, which releases us, and creates the water.

This Nothingness, this Not-self which we are, should not be misconstrued as meaning that there is no inherent conscious being: that the "individual point of view" is an illusion, that it does not exist. The philosopher David Hume (b.1771, d.1776) discovered that when he searched his mind for his self-consciousness, he could find nothing but perceptions, and nothing which he could determine as the owner of the perceptions, and therefore concluded that there is no innate conscious person but only an agglomeration of impressions. Buddhist as well have echoed this experience regarding the Buddha's Not-self doctrine, noting that all that is perceived is impermanent phenomena and never one who is discerning, no innate being, or individual entity. But this is like someone coming out of an empty room and claiming that there was no one there, not realizing that there was at least one person in the room. *In all observations there is always the indubitable point of view of the one who is observing; a perception cannot perceive itself. In every observation there is always "someone" who is looking at something.*

The assumption that nothing exists beyond the illusion of the Self is not only full of contradictions, but it degrades any sense of human meaningfulness to an irreconcilable nihilism. That is, just because you don't feel the plane moving at 550 mph does not mean that it is not going anywhere—and who would remain in an airplane that's going nowhere, anyway. In other words, if there is no actual human-being, if our sense of existence as individuals is an illusion, then anything and everything we do is absolutely absurd, meaningless, valueless. For, can any kind of value system be based on a physical matter, on an illusion of individuality, on an organic robot? An individual composed with organic matter, or an interrelation of conditions, or "emptiness" is really nothing but these being-less materials and conditions; it is REALLY nothing; it is ultimately valueless. To think otherwise is make-believe. It is very easy to slip from this perspective into nihilism, apathy, or depression. This is, in effect, the great error of our times: that by seeing everything through the glasses of reason, we have grown insensitive to the experience of raw existing, we have painted our Being-ness into a corner, that is, into non-existence. The fact is that there needs to be SOMEONE to observe that the Self is an illusion. I am a Nothingness because I am empty of the World, not because I do not exist.

This consciousness which I am, what would be my true self, I cannot see, because I am the one looking. Yet I know I am. In fact, the only thing of which I can be sure of is that I exist, and as we will see later, this certitude of existence is a fullness of Being. Everything that pops into the mind, be it thoughts, emotions, memories, or perceptions of our body or of our environment, is transitory, impermanent, and not a true self—and it pops back out. The experience of Being, however, is undeniable, it is indubitable: if anything IS, then I AM.

Yet, to say that "you are not your thoughts," as it has been proclaimed by some pundits, is not exactly accurate. That the thoughts are not a "true self" does not mean that the thoughts are not mine, or do not come from me—where else would they come from? I put them there. I produce them as well as the very Self which I have created out of my contact-with and grasping of the World. In the same manner, the emotions which arise have been engendered by me out of my reactions to the World. They are not alien to me as some other entity, as if I possessed by them. The brain does not produce thoughts by itself, it is not self-activating, any more than my arm can move by itself. That thoughts seem to appear out of nowhere is due to the unmindful habit of thinking, in the same manner as I don't think when I move my arm to scratch an itch. We reach for the World out of our need to be something, and in doing so, we give rise to thoughts, perceptions, emotions, identity; yet to deny them as "not who I am" would leave us squirming in the emptiness of the Nothingness. When it is said that "thoughts, emotions, and body are not self," it correctly means that we have an objective point of view on these manifestations. The Not-self doctrine of the Buddha *points to* that absolute subjectivity which is not the Self.

But why not just be your Self? Why make so much of this? Why not just accept yourself as you are and be done with it?

The problem is that the Self does not really exist. Or conversely, you can become any Self you want if you practice at it enough; like an actor, you can become any personality (derived from the Latin *persona*, relating to mask, or acting) you wish: yet none will be authentically you: they will all be an impermanent, conditioned thing, a convention, and a liability. Perhaps you are a happy person, feeling well most of the time, largely untroubled, yet if your wellbeing depends on things, situations, or people, or a perception of who you are, then it is not sustainable. Ultimately, anything which is made out the ideas is liable to change, and it will be at risk from the aggression of the world: from the opinions of others, from the loss of career, unemployment, loss of family, loss of youth, illness, etc.

It is in our existential project to overcome our No-thingness by grasping the World, that we become dependent on and lost in the Self. The Self is like a costume which we construct and decorate out of our life experiences, then wear it believing that it is who we truly are. As we will see, it is the reliance on this Self which becomes the origin of our suffering and of what Sartre calls Bad Faith.

Who we are, is not the Self!

The Self

Although it seems that we refer to a single identity when we say "I'm hungry" or "I'm sick" or "I love you," we actually work with several egos, and none of them a real entity. We have a work ego, a party ego, a father ego, an ego with parents, etc.; several different ways in which we see ourselves and interact with others in the world. All these egos proceed from a central yet ambiguous sense of Me that we can designate as the Self.

The term Ego (meaning "I" in Latin) was used by the renowned psychoanalyst Sigmund Freud (n.1856, d.1939) to refer to the psychological structure of the personality responsible for self-consciousness and that also functions to mediate the energies of the Id and the Super-ego to conform with reality. However, in contemporary pop psychology "the ego" is used more simply to designate the concept of self-identity.

For persons who have not developed the discipline of observing their minds carefully, their personality manifests according to the deterministic model described by Freud. That is, the Id as the instinctive drive for the immediate gratification of desire with a corresponding drive to destroy any opposition; the Super-ego as the reservoir of energies aimed at enforcing the cultural and parental norms of ideal behavior, being the conscience; and the Ego, as the conscious entity charged with balancing the unconscious energies of Id and Super-ego with the realities of life. These three entities are described as behaving with autonomy and frequently in conflict: The Id often coercing the Ego, and the superego suppressing the urges of the Id and encouraging the Ego to behave appropriately. This psychological structure, however, is the outcome of the pre-reflective consciousness grasping and becoming these various psychological states. When the pre-reflective mind identifies with particular thoughts as the Ego, then the instincts and emotionally charged ideals seem to come out of nowhere, affecting behavior and thoughts as if from beyond conscious control, or as an unconsciousness. Thence, the personality and behavior of most persons manifests as deterministic, as if lacking free will, as if manipulated by unconscious forces.

When one develops the ability to observe the objects of consciousness as objects of consciousness, as things apart from the conscious point of view, then it is not difficult to observe that the Id, the Ego, and the Super-ego are all objects of the mind. Then we recognize the Id as the instinctual, raw energies emanating from the body as simple physical reactions of pleasure and pain, which we then appropriate with desire, or rejects with suffering. The Ego are the perceptions and concepts which we entertain about who we are; and the Super-ego are the emotionally charged ideals which we have assimilated undigested from our culture and from our parents. Unconsciousness then is only the lack of attention to the surging instincts, concepts, and ideals. These mental manifestations you can observe as objects in consciousness, at a distance from your conscious point of view, and as impermanent conditions which the mind can manage and release at will.

If you are walking through a supermarket, for example, and you see your favorite ice cream, you may experience a sudden urge to eat it—very quickly to the mind come the memories of the taste and the happiness you felt when eating it. However, there is nothing that can force your mind to buy it. You can freely decide to ignore the instinctual compulsion for sweet foods (the Id), or you can comply with the thoughts of sticking to a healthy diet (the Super-ego), or you can figure out how many calories you can save with other foods and decide to purchase the ice cream anyway (the Ego). These thoughts are mental objects which the pre-reflective mind, the awareness, is free to choose or reject. However, if you quickly seize the thought of the pleasure in eating the ice cream, you may impulsively purchase it, without considering your motivation or consequences, becoming a victim of your instinct for sweetness, and then feel guilt for doing so.

It is generally understood that in various social situations the ego adopts different *roles* (such as a teacher, or parent, spouse, judge, doctor, etc.). However, the term "role" is more indicative of deliberate intentions and actions, literally as in acting or playing a role. What is observed, rather, when persons interact in distinct social situations is the complete immersion into different personalities, with conscious and subconscious manifestations, or more exactly, as the assimilation of different egos. These alternate ways of behaving are then incorporated into a comprehensive perception of what it is to be oneself: what I designate as the Self. The Self and its ego functions are the result of a pre-reflective consciousness identifying with, or becoming, its mental objects. Conversely, a mind that has realized its point of view as distinct from its mental objects does operate in the world with true roles, that is, fully mindful of its actions and intentions as actions and intentions: without ego or self, reference.

The trend of modern psychology is generally oriented at a deterministic interpretation of behaviors and the personality, accepting as reality only what can be objectively observed or empirically tested. This overlooks, however, a whole universe of subjective human experience; it is like as trying to learn to drive a car by studying the engine. From such a perspective, young children can be regarded, as Freud proposed, as consisting of pure instinctual drive—like little organic robots. Yet, as any parent can appreciate, even a young infant already reflects a recognition, a preference, and an intention towards the environment and persons; what is rather, the open and receptive awareness untainted by thought, concerns, or memories: an unencumbered consciousness.

The Self is born when consciousness becomes entangled with the World: with the stress of existence, with the fear of others, with the knowledge of mortality. We generate our sense of Self when our consciousness makes contact with the World: with thoughts, perceptions, memories, bodily sensations, and the physical world. We can detect the emergence of our Self by being acutely aware of the thoughts which arise when making self-reference, but we even more poignantly perceive its presence when affected by the emotions. As we will further discover in the chapter on the emotions, when we are angry or sad, or joyous, we are reacting to the World as Self.

Suppose now that for epidemiological reasons you have been forced to live in isolation: without neighbors, without communication with others, with nothing to do—no T.V. or cell phone access. There are plenty of nuts and fruits around, you have seeds to start vegetable garden, there is a freshwater stream nearby, you have been given a small cabin with a comfortable bed. You no longer have a profession, no work to perform, you don't have a title in your name. They have left you there only to live the rest of your life, only to exist; nobody will come looking for you, nothing is going to change; nobody's going to read your memoirs. How do you see your Self now?

Since there's only you, you don't have to worry about your hairstyle, or interesting clothes, there are no parties to go to. You don't need a name. You have nothing to plan for in the future other than taking care of your garden.

In this situation, you are nothing but an awareness of existing; there are no plans, no hopes, no projects to rely on for a sense of self-esteem, no worries. At first you struggle against emptiness, against the loss of identity, against the impulse to have something to do, something to become, but then the mind settles down and opens to the peace and happiness of just existing. It is to this state of mind, empty of all things, that you can then bring the world of things: your family, occupation, your projects and possessions, existing as objects of your consciousness.

When you and I were young children, we lived like this. We had no prospect of a career, no sexual anxiety, no fear of illness or death; we accepted those who entered our lives without prejudice or agenda; we simply enjoy eating, colors, smells, music, and the company of others; we were happy with the experience of just existing. The rest of this book will convince you that this awareness of existing as if without a Self is not an emptiness or an impossibility, but a fundamental source of meaningfulness and happiness.

The Truth About Suffering

As soon as we are born, we begin our struggle against an incessantly hostile world. In contrast to the weightless, warm darkness of the womb, we are assailed by blinding white lights, the wet, cold skin, the continuous need to breathe, and the pains of hunger and of voiding. We cry against a world of discomforts and exigencies, finding only brief islands of repose along the way. We are born into a world of suffering, and yet, this is what is necessary.

Straining between fleeing from pain and yearning for pleasure we gradually come to realize a sense of being and a self-identity. In this, Others—mainly our parents—are crucial in the development of our self-integrity and self-esteem. The infant identifies his/her self-existence as his/her cries are met by a consistent response from the parents. The tender stroking defines the body, the soothing voice and the loving gaze reflect to the infant a being-there. The child left to cry, the hunger not satisfied, the skin not touched, the words not heard, all contribute to a deformed and unstable Self. Growing up lacking regular and consistent parental bonding, a child develops emotional instability and a dis-integrated self-perception; subsequently reacting to the world with unmeasured anger, or excessive dependency, or depression. Our suffering conditions our Self-awareness, and Self-awareness conditions our suffering.

As we grow older, we are faced with the challenges of a growing body, of developing social skills and confronting social aggression, of completing an education and gaining employment, the stress of finding a partner, then the worries of marriage and family life, the threats of illness, of failure, of addiction, the afflictions and despondency of old age, and the angst of ever-looming death. Yet each struggle and each challenge are a summons to a deeper understanding of life and a more profound sense of Being.

But why so much suffering?

We, the self-conscious beings, are the latest and the greatest in a long line of evolution, not only since the first air-breathing fish crawled on to dry land, but back to the beginning of time, to the Big Bang. For 20 billion years the universe of galaxies and their stars have been evolving and exploding, and in their wake creating the elements and minerals which make up our earth and our bodies. Our bodies are a precise mixture of energy from the sun, minerals from the soil, and water from the seas. We breathe gases from the atmosphere to keep our internal fire going. It is this continuous necessity to replenish the constituents of our bodies, which creates the incessant craving for the materials of the world. We are always lacking the world.

We also inherit an animal nature which has survived 20 million years in the struggle of kill or be killed and sex through conquest. While our technology and society advance exponentially, we drag along an ancient body with a mind still compelled by primitive survival instincts. Jealousy, greed, anger, aggression, selfishness, were the psychological weapons humanity forged in the primeval struggle for survival in a world with limited resources and an abundance of violence; yet these forces still dominate the minds of many in the present, even in societies with an overabundance of wealth and education. The overpowering primordial urge for reproduction still

17

in modern times blind and demonize hearts of many even to extreme perversions, causing bestial harm to the most helpless, and deceiving very educated persons. Because of the ignorance we still hold about the nature of the mind, we remain victims of these primitive forces and continue victimizing each other—creating deserts of salt in our lives. Humankind is still a chimera: aspiring to the heavens but with our roots still deep in the mud.

We are born into and constrained to thrive in a world of suffering. We need the world to survive, to quench our hunger, our thirst, our physical discomfort, and our boredom; and the lack of it causes our pains. We suffer the consequences of failing to control our primitive urges. Because we are born contingent on the world, we desire, and because we desire, we suffer. Our human condition is such that we are ruled by desire.

But it gets worse.

There are as many different desires as there are individuals, but what all desires have in common is an *existential lack*. By this lack, I am not only indicating a want for something which we don't have, but more significantly, a lack of an essence of being. My perception of who I am will always be lacking because I can never *see* who I truly am: I can never directly experience who I am: because viewed from the perspective of reflection, from thinking, I can only discern that I am not any-thing: I am a Nothingness.

The only thing which we can indubitably know about our existence is that we exist, and nothing else: But what is existence? As a result, we attempt to fill our existential emptiness with a Self which we create out of the World—to exist as something we can identify. This lack of essential identity conditions our strong desires, and the problem with desiring a World which is not me, which is not mine, is that I am always going to fail at creating a real and enduring Me. From an existential perspective, I will always be lacking an authentic Self, an authentic identity: It will always be some convention, some illusion of being.

18

This existential Lacking sometimes surfaces during times crisis, and sometimes following a significant life event, yet much more commonly as *boredom*. Boredom usually strikes in our solitude, in the quiet peacefulness of a lazy afternoon, or during a long weekend when there is nothing good to watch on the television, and you can't find anyone to go out with, and you are tired of doing puzzles and reading; then we are confronted by a slow burgeoning restlessness, a vague feeling of emptiness, a meaninglessness, as symptoms of the disintegration of the Self. Here, when there is nothing to do, nothing to grasp at hand, we suddenly experience a widening of the abyss between our being-ness and the world; then abruptly, we find ourselves, as Sartre puts it, suspended in Nothingness.

It is the Nothing, Heidegger explains, which makes human Being possible: it is the foundation of self-consciousness. Yet, the spontaneous manifestation of the Nothing is unnerving for most of us. Most turn away from this epiphany and anxiously reach for the things of the world to fill this void: with shopping, with eating, with exercise, by keeping the mind busy with electronic devices or long work hours, some tragically by self-medicating with drugs or alcohol, and some turning to thrill-seeking or infidelity in order to "feel alive." But, since the pleasures of the world are not lasting, we can only, at best, experience a temporary satisfaction, a passing reprieve from this boredom, and are soon to be burdened again to seek more distraction. Some become chronically afflicted with this existential restlessness, succumbing to depression or addictions. Although religion can to a great extent provide fulfillment by fostering a spiritual identity—as a being which is beyond the world—for most people the engagement is typically not profound enough to induce a transcendence of suffering.

If we factor in world hunger and malnutrition, diseases, accidents, homicide and suicide, mental illness, physical and emotional abuse, sexual abuse, and wars, we can accurately state that life, for most of the people in the world, is about the pains and struggles of survival. Few if any could say that life is meaningful because it is beautiful and pleasurable. Rather, we find meaning for our lives despite excessive suffering.

But what exactly is suffering?

Although frequently associated with the sensation of pain, the term suffering is more appropriately used to signify psychological pain. All animals feel pain, and, as a herald of injury, it is lifesaving. However, only us, the self-conscious animals, react to pain with existential fear: a fear of Self-injury or impending annihilation. We suffer because we believe that the body which we identify with the Self or the thoughts and emotions which we recognize as Self are existentially threatened. We fear for our Self when we can't get what we want, or when we don't want what we have.

The Buddha identified *craving* as the essential cause of suffering (the Third Noble Truth): craving for sensual pleasures, craving for existence, and craving for non-existence (DN 22). But these are the symptoms of the more fundamental condition of existential lack: our desire to fill our Nothingness with the World as Self. We crave the World to assert and sustain the Self, and we reject that which threatens it. Ultimately, it is our essential Nothingness which conditions our desires, and consequently conditions our sufferings.

Because the human mind has not inherent nature, no essence, it will become at once the objects it holds conscious. Which means that if you go around all day reviewing negative thoughts, your mind will grow heavy and weary, unhappy (salty); or, if you maintain pleasant and positive thoughts then you will feel light and joyful, and happy (fluid). For the same reason, as we will further learn in other chapters, our emotions, attitudes, and actions toward others will as well condition our own happiness.

We suffer because we are self-conscious of pain and because we know what it means not-to-be, but we suffer precisely because it is a condition for our freedom. It is our suffering the world which *extricates* us from the world, which identifies materiality as other-than-me. Therefore, suffering is not an absurd or avoidable condition of our existence, but rather fundamentally necessary for our emancipation. If we were not free of the world, we would be like the other animals: identified with the world to the point of un-self-consciousness. We would feel and avoid pain, but it would not be personal, not suffering. It is because the Self is not who we effectively are, that we are not constrained by the world—that our consciousness is not totally absorbed into it. Suffering is the price we paid for our self-consciousness: It is our eviction from the Garden of Eden. The irony is, that even though we are not the Self we create, and it becomes the contingency for our suffering, we are nevertheless dependent on this creation to become individual autonomous beings.

If we had everything our way, if we did not need to strive for anything, if we did not have to suffer the world, we would not mature, for our complacency would leave us undeveloped. We see examples of this in the infant with delayed walking due to being carried too much, with the bored, spoiled teenager, or in the syndrome of the overprotected child. Many parents fear the stress of having to punish, and as a result, their children do not internalize self-control and later have problems with self-discipline and socialization, leading to a cascade of lifelong failures. Other parents, wanting to shield their children from any form of physical or emotional discomfort, keep them from experiencing any stress and do everything for them. Because these parents dread having to suffer the suffering of their children, the children become adults with a great fear of being hurt, unable to handle and manage failure and rejection, and unable to put up with discomfort and prolonged effort, in the long run their suffering becomes much the worse. It is precisely the having to suffer the world, the hunger, which keeps us moving and growing —what gets us out of bed each morning.

But how, or by what means, is it that we suffer?

Suffering is a psychological pain. Surprisingly, many scientists who study pain believe that psychological pain does not exist: It is not real because there is no physical damage to the brain—i.e., if you can't see it in an MRI, it doesn't exist (Biro 2010). But just take candy away from a young child, and you will see psychological pain in all its glory. Indeed, anyone who has lost a loved one will relate how mental suffering is the worst kind of pain, because it is relentless—if you are conscious, it is there—despite not having any physical brain injury.

But what causes psychological pain?

If you sit in a quiet area, with your eyes closed, and observe your mind, you will soon see how you grasp or reject the thoughts which appear to your awareness. A thought arises of something pleasant, like an ice cream cone or an attractive person, and you want to keep the image present in mind to experience the pleasure it produces, so you make a mental effort to keep remembering it. When we want something, we focus our attention on it as if grabbing it with the mind. Now, imagine there is a fly in the ice cream, and you quickly want to get rid of the image by thinking of something else. When there is something we don't like, we as if push it away in the mind, we strain against it or try to suppress the thought of it with something else, and this causes mental discomfort and stress. *Mental pain* then occurs when we *reject* a thought which we at the same time *sustain* in mind: we genuinely want it there, because it is important for us, but at the same time it causes us distress, and so we also want to get rid of it. So, if I have lost a loved one, I want to keep the object of my desire in mind, but the thought of the loss threatens my existence, so I want to get rid of it— "how can I live without her." On the other hand, if I have been insulted, I reject the thought of the insult, but at the same time I want to keep it in mind to fight against it, to rationalize it in my favor, because it threatens to overwhelm my self-integrity—"how could she say that to me!" What maintains conflict active, what keeps it alive, is the emotional energy we give it. Mental pain is this simultaneous holding on and rejection, what strains and exhausts the mind. If the focus of the desire, the thought or emotion, suddenly goes away (as while entertaining some other activity), so does the suffering. However, even though we can suppress a thought, by forcing it out of mind by focusing on another idea, if it has not been resolved, its emotional energy will keep it imminent.

Suffering ferments out of our Nothingness. Confronted with our essential emptiness, we mold a Self out of the stuff of the World; to sustain this Self, we hunger for the body, hunger for pleasures, and for existence; but because the Self is an impermanent condition, and foreign to our essence, we unceasingly suffer and fear its disintegration. Ultimately then, we suffer because of our attachment to the Self.

The truth about suffering is that it exists as a result of our human condition, it is inescapable, and it is necessary. It is suffering which initially levers the extrication of our being from the world— in realizing a not-being the world—and then consolidates our consciousness of a Self. It is through our personal suffering by which we become individual human beings: an individual Self. It is also suffering which fosters our development and maturation, what gets us out of bed, and what builds character. But even more, it is suffering which inspires us to transcend the world, to realize our absolute Freedom.

Life will always be a lacking-of; life will come to meet every one of us with challenges, obligations, and responsibilities; life will be frequently uncomfortable, and often painful. This is just the way things are. We suffer much more when we crave and reject, when we fear pain, and fear for the Self. We also suffer even more because we fear to suffer. We fear the suffering of a relationship, the suffering of work, the suffering of the body, the suffering of growing old, the suffering of our children; and in the running away from this fear we divorce, indulge in endless entertainment, repudiate the body, and overprotect or neglect our children.

By grasping our fear of suffering, we fail to realize that overcoming difficulties makes us stronger and indolence makes for atrophy. It is the struggle that strengthens our bodies and toughens the mind. Suffering is not to be feared; it is to be understood, accepted, and transcended.

Desiderata

We are condemned to desire. Because we are subject to physical existence, because we are a Nothingness and lack essential nature, we must desire, and we must choose.

But what we most desire is happiness. Our desire for happiness is at the root of all other intentions. While we might wish for better health, success, more money, more time, the recovery or wellbeing of others, or not having family problems, the underlying aspiration is for our personal satisfaction. And while we NEED many things for our survival and health, we WANT many more which we believe will make our Self happier. Whereas a desire out of necessity ensues out of contingency, like wanting food because you are hungry; a desire out of want issues from a dependence on Self, e.g., wanting a doughnut. The desire which engenders from the Self, however, will only breed disappointment.

As we have already seen, we are *thrown* into a world of necessities and suffering. It is the lack of what we need to survive and the distress which ensues, that condition our desires for the material world. We NEED food for our hunger, water for our thirst, clothing, shelter to protect us from the environment, and each other for our sense of existence.

Suspended in warm amniotic fluid, the consciousness of the fetus is unbothered, centered, and peaceful. With birth, the body comes into the awareness, with the cold, the wet, the hunger, the pains. The warm blankets, the milk feeding, the soothing voices, are a respite from the aggressions of physical existence, inciting our yearnings for the pleasures of the world. Our life is a searching, a lacking, a craving, a becoming, a journey of self-discovery and self-creation, driven by the austerities of life and the brevity of satisfaction, fueled by desires.

It is by means of the body by which we interact in the world, and therefore it becomes the keystone in the development and evolution of the Self.

Consciousness contacts the universe through the senses, manifesting as pleasant or unpleasant reactions and instigating our likes and dislikes; but we do not encounter the sensation itself, rather the chocolate, the perfume, the silk blouse, the cold rain. As well, I do not move my arm to grasp something, rather I reach for the hammer, I play the piano; I do not move one leg after the other, but I walk and I dance: the body is experienced as Me. Not only do we extend out into the world across the body, but also the body becomes at once the expression and affirmation of our personal existence. This we clearly witness in the joie de vivre displayed by young children with the movement of their bodies, in their elation with singing, running, dancing. I say "I am hungry," or "I am thirsty," or "I am cold," because after so many years of experiencing life in the body, it feels like Me. I am tall, I am old, I am 5 years old, I am Asian, white, or black, I am a man, I am a woman: This body, I feel is my Self.

Yet how well do we know this body?

If you sit in a quiet place and focus on the immediate sensations of the body, you would feel the pressure produced by gravity on the buttocks and soles of the feet, the weight of your hands resting

on the laps, some lower back muscle tension from the sitting position, perhaps the coolness of exposed skin and light feel of clothing, or maybe an itch or intestinal discomfort; you would have
made an effort to be aware of the movement of the breath or the
blinking of the eyes. You would not notice, however, the dynamic
beating of your heart 70 times per minute and the movement of
blood from the large arteries to every single microscopic capillary
and cell. Unaware of the kidneys filtrating 45 gallons of blood daily
and regulating your blood pressure and the minerals of the blood
to a decimal of a difference. You would be insensitive to the diges-
tion and absorption of food by your 25 feet of intestine, the hun-
dreds of chemical reactions occurring in the liver, and the production and regulation of dozens of hormones by the body glands. The
reality is that we are unconscious to most of our organ systems and
ignorant of the vast complex processes which take place daily for
our bodies to survive another day. Furthermore, if you could see
them, you would not recognize your heart or kidney as different
from that of another person of your same height. In other words,
I am my body little more than I am my car.

Yet, on the other hand, the body is more than just a vessel,
more than a machine, not an avatar. It is primarily by means of the
human body through which a consciousness accomplishes an individual self-conscious existence, and by which we achieve an objective being-ness. This results in a predicament because I need this
body to be Me, and yet this body is not Me, it is not who I am.
When my hopes for happiness are projected onto my body or the
body of others, then I will unavoidably suffer, because my body
and other bodies, and the ideas of bodies, are objects of my consciousness; the body is not what I truly am.

In pursuing our Self-satisfaction through the desire of our
body, we create the body image as a concept of what the body looks
like to us, and what it looks like to others. Concerning the latter,
there is a myriad of manufacturers who spend a lot of money to

convince us that their product will make us more attractive and thus happier—and we spend a lot of money believing them. With every purchase of makeup, clothing, diet and exercise products, we aspire for the attention and admiration of others, and long for the happiness and self-fulfillment we hope it will bring. This endeavor, however, will invariably meet with frustration due your inaccurate perception of your body image and of the body itself, and of what others happen to communicate to you. Since our point of view has a subjective perspective on the body, we have difficulties creating an accurate, objective body image: we are constrained to see ourselves through the eyes of the beholder. As Sartre pointed out, we precisely transcend the body: We don't see it, we live it. We are dependent on others to give us the body we desire. Evidence of this is the many times we are duped into believing that some article of clothing or accessory will look as good on us as on a model. As a result, we are always liable to an obscured self-image and the biases of others. For example, you're walking down the street and an attractive person smiles at you and you feel pretty, or handsome, and happy, then a few minutes later your friend points out the red smudge on your nose, and you feel foolish. If your happiness depends on what others think of you, then you will always be lacking, you will always be prone to suffer.

We desire the body of others to satisfy the instinct for sex. Although the desire for sex appears to arise from the Self—that is, it seems as Me or mine—in effect it originates from the body, from the urge of nature. Our appetite for sex, if observed mindfully, is not very different from our appetite for food. We may not be very hungry, but suddenly we get a whiff of some well-seasoned food and we begin to salivate. We don't perceive the body as hungry, but rather "I am hungry"—we appropriate the hunger as Self. After we eat, it is not the body which is perceived as satisfied, but Me. It is the same with the sexual appetite: it originates from the body, but we appropriate the urge and the pleasure as Me and mine.

Sexual desire is one of our strongest instincts, second only to the fear of death; and in the same manner as the body, we think we own it but most of the time it owns us. Sex, as the primeval energy of creation, is as old as life itself. Indeed, we call it an instinct because it drives the mind as if by taking possession of it. It is bewildering how very educated and mature individuals will risk almost everything—reputation, family, career—for a sexual encounter. The intense energies generated amplify our sense of being a body and of existing: make you feel "alive". However, like everything else from the body, as not being Me nor mine, it will eventually prove a frustration and a liability to a fulfilling happiness. The accurate truth is that sex is stressful, it demands a large investment of personal energy and time, and is full of social risks and emotional complications, and it is potentially full of salt.

Our desire for existence, our desire to exist as an object for oneself, beckons us to grasp the world and each other across the body. Although, as the Buddha taught, it is desire which conditions our suffering, our desire for the body and the world, as we have seen, originates essentially from an existential fear of non-being. It is the emptiness, the void, generated by the Nothingness of consciousness, that engenders the hunger for a Self, for an objective existence, for a material being-ness as a body.

The Self formed out of a body which we barely know and little control, and contingent on an impermanent world, becomes an unstable and elusive thing that must be kept alive through desire. When we desire the world to sustain our Self, then the things we need become the things we WANT. Then instead of the food we need for our proper nutrition, we want junk food to placate the boredom and quell the emptiness. Instead of comfortable clothing to protect us from the environment, we want expensive designer garments to impress and influence others. Rather than spending time with friends, we want to be associated with people who will feed our egos or ambitions through their status or wealth. All the things that we want for our Self—wealth, power, and fame—will always leave us restless and hungry for something more which will fill the emptiness and allay our unhappiness.

While we search the world for our satisfaction, what we truly desire is fulfillment; that some-thing which will fill the emptiness of our lives with meaning and true happiness.

The Emotional Me

Emotions seem to be the spice of life, and while an emotionless-life would seem not very appealing, when observed closely and realistically, our emotions turn out to be more like too much Tabasco in your soup or too much sugar in your coffee.

Although emotions come in a great variety of flavors, they all stem from a combination of four basic primitive psychological reactions, namely: anger, sadness, joy, and fear. In the same manner that the four basic tastes (sour, sweet, salty, and bitter) constitute the great variety of flavors, a combination these basic reactions comprise the great variety of other emotions. Disgust, for example, is a combination of fear and anger; excitement is a mixture of fear and joy. The four basic emotional reactions are instinctive, or primitive, as they originate from a primal part of the brain termed the *limbic system,* also called the paleomammalian cortex. We experience emotions physically because the activity of the limbic system is highly connected with other parts of the brain and the regulation of hormones. These are then reflected in the body causing feelings of: chest tightness, hyperventilation, sweating, butterflies in the stomach, headache, giddiness, and many more.

Theories of emotions in general describe the body reaction, or arousal, as occurring first in response to a stimulus, like a reflex reaction, which is then perceived consciously as the emotion; that is, the emotion is a secondary reaction to the arousal. Accordingly, we feel afraid because we feel the trembling (the arousal) of the body first, as a response to the external stimulus (a snake). Apparently, the primitive limbic system recognizes the danger and reacts before we are even conscious of it. These observations and interpretations, however, fail to notice the role of the pre-reflective consciousness as what first recognizes and reacts to the external stimulus, occurring at such rapid speed that it appears as instinctive or unconsciously. Precisely, there is the initial pre-reflective recognition of danger to the Self (the external stimulus), then the instinctive physiological reflex reaction to danger (the limbic reaction), and finally the reflective verbal affirmation of the event (the recognition of the emotion). This initial pre-reflective recognition can be appreciated to be fully conscious, and rapid, with some training in mindful awareness of the mind: for example, first you discern (pre-reflectively) that the car in front has suddenly stopped, then very quickly (pre-reflectively) you asses the danger and what you need to do, by trained muscle reflex you hit the brakes, then your heart starts to thump (the limbic danger reaction), and finally the emotional recognition that your life was in mortal danger. If it were otherwise you would freeze in your fear, not knowing what to do, and be too late to step on the brake; that is, the limbic system itself cannot figure out what is happening, or that you need to step on the brakes.

Most of the research on emotions these days look to detect with imaging the effect the emotions have on the structures of the brain, or involve objective observations of human behavior, or extrapolate from behavior experiments on rats. These objective, evidence-based, deterministic studies of emotions, and human behavior in general, are (again) like trying to figure out how drive a car by studying the engine or trying to learn how to swim by studying fish. No doubt emotions arise from the activity of the brain structures, but here, rather, it is a conscious being who manipulates the structures of the brain—much in the same way we use a computer—not the other way around.

Psychologically, the subjective experience of emotions can be categorized according to the intention the mind expresses towards an object, respectively: grasping for joy, rejection for fear, positive reaction to obstruction for anger, and negative reaction to obstruction for sadness. The intentions, in turn, are derived from the nature of the Self. If I create a desire for something—a sugary warm fresh doughnut, for example—and my wish is fulfilled, I feel joy; if I remember that I am watching my weight and resist my urges, then I may feel sadness; if a coworker takes the doughnut away to help me with my diet, I will feel anger; and if my doctor tells me that doughnuts will clog my arteries, then fear. Therefore, my primitive emotions are triggered by my conscious reactions for Self-preservation when threatened by an environmental stimulus, as they have for the past thousands of years—the coworker now playing the role of the wolf stealing away the rabbit I caught. It is in this respect that the emotions which helped us survive the primitive earth, are now excessive for our present state of existence.

Although our emotions help us to manage the aggressions and frustrations of the world, more frequently they erupt out of our attachment to the Self, out of a psychological threat to our Self; that is, most of the time we are fighting and fleeing our ideas.

Anger, the fire of the mind fueled by the sympathetic nervous system and the release of adrenalin made it possible for us to stand tall against the saber tooth tiger and the ancient grisly. While there are no tigers and bears threatening our physical existence these days, we employ the same powerful reaction against whatever threatens our Self. We use our anger to protect our self-esteem, our reputation, our body image, our heritage, which would seem like a good thing, except that what we end up fighting against most of the time are our own thoughts.

Anger, however, is always an existential reaction to fear, the fear of injury to the body or the Self. Those who have had a to live with poverty, fight the fear of being without, of lacking; those who have been ignored fight the fear of being nothing, of not being valued. If we identify with a vulnerable ego, then we tend to be angry often, lashing out at whoever threatens our ideology, our habits, our self-image, our self-righteousness. The anger reaction is initially a pre-reflective recognition of a danger to the Self—again, occurring so rapidly in the mind that it seems as if subconscious—then the instinctive reaction of the paleomammalian brain, and subsequently emotional response and sensation in the body. If anger becomes a habit, if it becomes a Self-identity, then one will be continuously exposed to the toxic effects of adrenaline, and the psychological and physical effects of excessive stress, such as immunosuppression, hypertension, anxiety, and depression.

Anger feels heavy on the mind, it is irritating, stiffening; you can't dance the twist, tell a joke, laugh, or care for others when you are angry. The Self of a frequently angry person is unhappy. The truth is that anger is more toxic to the Me than threatening anyone else; the more ire we throw at others, the more it builds up in us; over time growing like a cancer, overpowering and clouding the mind.

When our intention to grasp or reject an object is frustrated, and we are overwhelmed, and we experience sadness. When we judge that threat of injury to the Self is overwhelming, then we retreat, we hide; when the frustration to obtain what we want is too great, then we feel defeated, depressed. Sadness is a retraction of the mind into itself; it is weak, dull, helpless. When we are sad, we withdraw our attention from the world; we are absent-minded, unaware of the most beautiful sunny day. While anger confronts the world in simple terms, sadness blends into many shades: from sympathy, to melancholy, to depression.

Sadness is one of the ways we suffer the World. Sadness results from our bonding to the World, from our desire of things and others, and it is the straining or breaking of this bond which causes the pain of suffering. Yet ironically, the fear of sadness is what keeps us together, what sustains the bond; that is, if drifting apart did not cause pain of loss, a grieving, then it would be effortless to break our relationships. The avoidance of sadness keeps families together and lovers involved. As sympathy, it inspires us to care for the weak, the elderly, and the helpless. It promotes the cohesion of groups, cultures, and nation. Love brings us together, but sadness keeps us from drifting apart.

Sadness is about desire, about attachment, about longing, and the more we have been attached to something or someone, the greater will be the sorrow and pain of losing. Sadness heals with time, as a desire burns out through habituation or disinterest. However, if the longing has been too great or lasting too long, then the sadness itself becomes the object of attachment. Although there are many things which can provoke a major depression—hormone imbalance, tragic loss, a severe physical injury—when the sadness itself becomes a constant focus of attention, then the original stimulus fades into the background as the Self is overtaken by sadness, as sadness becomes a depression. What underscores depression is the fear of emptiness, the fear of not being anything: since being sadness is better than being nothing at all.

We feel the emotion of joy when a desire is fulfilled; when the longing, the anxiousness, the fear of being without, or the fear of emptiness, is relieved. Yet, however bright the joy may be, its shadow is always sadness, always the fear of loss, of being empty again. For this reason, joy can never amount to happiness, as it always lingers with a bit of fear.

Instead than making life more interesting, grasping our primitive emotions, like too much Tabasco or too much salt, rather overwhelms the natural flavors life. Emotions are a response to underlying fear: fear of not getting what we want (sadness and anger), and fear of losing what we have (joy and sadness). Emotions come into being from the grasping the World as Self. As we will see, Authentic Happiness does not hinge on anything, it is transparent, it is fearless, desire-less, transcending all primitive emotions.

Fear of Freedom

Fear, as a reaction to danger, is ubiquitous of all living beings; it keeps us alive. But to be truly afraid you must be self-conscious; you must be able to anticipate your non-existence. We humans are the only animals that fear death. We are the only animals that know what it means to not exist, who know the Nothing: the being Nothing. Our *essentia* as Nothingness not only makes us fear physical death, but also feeds our dread of being no-one.

Existential fear is not like the distressful reaction to an in-your-face fiend. It is a fear of the unknown, as despair, an anxiety, as angst; like a dark night, the Nothingness negates our very identity, bringing us face to face with the possibility of our non-existence. Although we are occasionally confronted with the crude reality of our mortality, as when ill or witnessing someone's death, most of the time we go out of our way to avoid thinking about it. To this extent, we create fantasies about who we are and what our life is all about, to hide the abominable truth: that we have no idea of why we exist, of why we know that we exist, and that we are going to die. We turn away and grasp the Self in disavowal of the apprehension that death makes our existence absurd: that our life is about

Nothing. And while most of us find some solace in the belief in God, the call to Faith is testimony to a silent relationship.

The sudden encounter with our Nothingness can be dizzying, sometimes unnerving, and sometimes terrifying, not only because we find ourselves suspended over an abysmal emptiness, but because we further realize that there is nothing holding us up: that this Nothingness is also an absolute Freedom. As a Nothingness, since I exist as a point of view outside of the World, as if at a distance from it, I am essentially unconditioned by it; even more, I am the one who makes the World come to be. From my point of view of not being anything, I am entirely free to be anything. Ironically, as Sartre noted, we are afraid of our Freedom. We are afraid of the responsibility and liability of being unconstrained. We are fearful of losing control because there is nothing controlling us, nothing for us to hold on to. Evidence to this radical freedom of the mind is the unpredictable behavior of human beings: ranging from the most sublime compassion and selfless kindness, to the most unimaginable callousness and cruelty—and we never fail to be astonished at the extent of human viciousness. Unlike the animals, there are no natural boundaries to restrict human behavior, nothing intrinsic to stop us from acts of cruelty, murder, or suicide. It is because of the fear we have of this unconditioned mind, in the knowledge of what it is capable of, that we need strong taboos, laws, and punishments as deterrents.

This existential Freedom becomes most conspicuous and threatening when in solitude. When we are alone, we are free from the judgments of others, but we are thereof lacking a reflection of our being: there is no one out there objectifying our existence. Here, the Nothingness manifests as an absolute subjectivity, and absolute Freedom. Yet for one who is attached to the Self, this estranging power is more often revealed as angst, or as per Sartre, as existential nausea. Hence, we may feel as if disoriented, unable to put our finger on what we are supposed to be doing, feeling as alien to our-Self. To escape the Nothingness, many seek self-identity in a lifestyle, in groups, institutions, ideologies, gangs, or cults. However, what defines us also limits us, and so we build a gilded cage around us by forsaking our Freedom for the sake of security; we act in Bad Faith.

The question of free will has been fodder for the contemplations and discussions of philosophers since the ancient Greeks. The answer bears importance, not only for how accountable we are for our decisions and their consequences—for example, as to whether an individual who committed a premeditated crime had full liberty to choose a course of action, or was instead a victim of his/her genes and circumstances—but more important, as to whether we are able to alter our fate and freely choose our destiny. Arguments in this respect are numerous and complex, ranging from the materialists and determinists, proposing that human behavior to be wholly determined by material forces (like organic robots), to the deists, and theists, arguing for the autonomy and spirituality of beings, yet all characterized by the inconclusiveness of their postulations.

Nonetheless, the vast majority of us are not free and are gravely unaware of the nature and power of our essential Freedom. As we have already noted, we are strongly affected, and at times enslaved, by our animalistic drives of lust and aggression. Our thoughts and emotions are as well conditioned by our life experiences, the quality of our upbringing, and our innate sensibilities. We generally and indiscriminately accept notions and attitudes from our parents and our culture, with respect to what is acceptable or normal. We heedlessly follow socially defined scripts for handling many situations in our daily life: from the way we greet, converse, eat, and dispose of our secretions. We maintain elaborate internal dialogs to help us control ourselves and remember our self-identity. Thus, for the average person, in the humdrum of day-to-day existence, the will-power is very much conditioned, having little awareness of the forces which influence our intentions and actions.

However, although there are many factors which influence our decisions, intuitively we are also very much aware of our freedom to choose. At the supermarket, at mealtimes, when picking out an outfit or a television channel, we consider our options and make decisions, never surprised by our choices—as we would be if not in full in control of our intentions. Furthermore, even if preferences were the direct product of internal and external conditions, the factors which determine even simple human behavior are so complex and varied, that for all practical purposes conform more to a theory of chaos than determinism.

Despite biases, what impresses our sense of autonomy is the intuition of the disconnection of our point of view from the various possibilities for behavior. Like Neo in the last sequel of *The Matrix* when he confronts the Architect and observes himself in each of the many monitor screens displaying different emotional reactions, we similarly consider in our mind alternative reactions in response to a given situation. For example, in deciding whether to eat a donut or an apple, I may consider my present weight, my cholesterol, the social environment (are others choosing donuts), my childhood experiences with apples and donuts, my impulse control, the appearance of the food, among other factors—and then if a coworker suggests choosing the apple, I may pick the opposite out of spite or accept counsel. All these options run through the mind very quickly, seemingly subconsciously, yet the options are *out there* for my consideration: I can see them mindfully as different possibilities for a response.

If you observe your mind carefully, you can see that, when you consider to make a decision, it is thoughts and emotions which you contemplate in making your selection, while the act of deciding itself is unconditioned. So, in making a random selection between pressing a red or green button, for example, without knowing the consequences of either choice, you might be inclined to choose green because it is more environmental color, or your favorite color, and not red because it's the color of blood; yet all these thoughts appear as other options to choose from. You would be able to make an absolute random decision if you are mindful of not accepting any bias; that is, if you just see the colors as meaningless colors. The decision is just complex, but not predetermined or subconscious, if you are mindful.

Our Nothingness is the necessary condition for our existential Freedom (or free will) and our Self-identity. Which means that it is because my life is about nothing, because nothing is conditioning me, that I can exercise an absolutely free will in deciding who I want to see my-Self as. And yet, it is also this profound, unnerving Freedom as a Nothingness which leads to the grasping of a Self, and what makes it so daunting to let it go.

It is the forsaking of this essential Freedom which Sartre calls Bad Faith. We always grasp the Self in Bad Faith. It is the fear of absolute Freedom, as the existential expression of our Nothingness, which coerces us to grasp the Self with the ambition of forging an existential solidity: to be something. That is, we are afraid not be anything. Alas, this venture will always fail on account of the fragile nature of any Self. In pretending to be something we are not, there will always be some misstep, some unforeseen misfortune, which hurls us back into the Nothing; there will always be a lack of authenticity, an unfulfillment, a dissatisfaction. In forsaking our unconditioned Freedom for an elusive sense of Self, we are like Esau, exchanging our birthright to a kingdom for a bowl of salty soup.

The Others

In his masterwork *Being and Nothingness,* Sartre keenly illustrated the encounter with the Other. He depicts a man looking through a keyhole in a dark hallway. Wholly absorbed in his activity, he is lost to any sense of self-awareness, he is solely his peeping. Then suddenly, he hears steps approaching, and abruptly becomes aware of his being there, of his existing, and of the fact that he is a voyeur. By this mental experiment, Sartre demonstrated the complex interaction between conscious beings: the ever-circular interplay of self-as-subject for itself, and self-as-object for the Other.

When we look at an inanimate object, we perceive it as just that: a three-dimensional object in space. However, when we are confronted by a conscious being, we become acutely aware of another dimension, an inner dimension: the dimension of consciousness. This inner dimension, whether of an animal or a human, is an enigma for us, and it is fearful because it is unpredictable; it can suddenly turn on us. Although nonliving things can be unpredictable—such as a storm, lightning, a sinkhole—these are not confrontational, not directed at me personally. We can get lost in thought while watching a tree, flowers, or a statue, as objects of our consciousness. But when approached by something with an inner-dimension, I suddenly realize myself an object for another subject—and this becomes something which is now out of my hands. The universe is no longer just represented in my consciousness, there is another universe for which I am an object. What Sartre described as the Look of the Other is that power of consciousness that we know all too well but are pressed to describe; because it is for us another Nothingness. The Look of the Other provokes as much angst as my own Nothingness; and yet, we also yearn for this Look because it is the only time when I can have a realization of my own objectiveness: I want the Other to recognize this unique being which is Me.

We can particularly recognize the effect of the Other when in competition. Then, I become acutely sensitive to that other consciousness confronting Me. It is interesting to note that organized chess competitions between humans and computers are largely unpopular. Even though a computer can be adjusted to any level of play, and it is very difficult for a chess Grand Master to beat a computer, hardly anyone experiences great thrill playing against a silicon brain. Rather, it is when sitting across a chess board against another consciousness that we feel confronted and the adrenaline starts to rush, causing the excitement which draws thousands to competition. Computer against computer chess matches are sometimes held with the attraction being the designer of the best thinking engine—reminiscent of competitions a century ago when thousands would gather to watch the head-on collision of large steam locomotives. It is the awareness of the consciousness of the Other, and the interplay of feelings and emotions, which is both a threat and a passion in human interaction.

No human grows up alone. We are all as children dependent on Others to feed us, clothe us, protect us, and inform us of the world;

even more, to inform us of our own existence, of our sense of being. Without an Other, a person would be little more self-conscious than an animal: one would not be human, as Sartre asserts.

Especially in relationships, we are beholden to the Other to give us what we can't see; and sometimes we sell our freedom cheap to gain a little bit of Me. Since we occupy a subjective point of view on the world, and since we *live* our body but cannot realistically see it, we are obliged to Others to give us information as to how we are perceived, and even as to who we are. However, in giving this power to the Others, we diminish our own subjective-ness and our freedom; and as a result, we become vulnerable. Contrarily, in lessening the importance of the Others we lessen their subjective-ness, in seeing them more as objects, but this then obscures our own objective-ness. As Sartre further explains, this creates a power struggle without any easy resolution; making personal relationships as much threatening as alluring, and rarely unambiguous.

We are obliged to Others to help us create our Self, but to this extent become vulnerable to their prejudices. As we grow into adulthood, we are given perceptions and values about people and the world which we assimilate unquestioned and unexamined. We adopt these ideas and beliefs as part of what it means to be Me. We thoughtlessly accept opinions regarding correct physical appearance, clothing, and behavior, which we employ to discriminate others, or to criticize ourselves when we cannot live up to our own expectations.

But our personal interactions affect us even more precariously. Because *everything we do unto others we also do unto our Self*—what we might call the Red Rule of Morality. The reason for this reciprocal effect is that every intention will affect the Self with the same condition, because every action is a projection of the absolute-subjective state. This means, for example, that to be angry at someone you first are constrained to create anger within you, and this becomes a condition the mind will then grasp as Self. Likewise, an act of kindness must proceed from the loving-kindness that wells within you. When an emotion takes hold of the mind, like anger or sadness, the mind becomes absorbed in it for a duration; it becomes the emotion for a while. The more we practice the grasping of a behavior, an idea, or an emotion, the more it becomes our way of being; the more it becomes what I identify as my-Self. This reciprocal effect occurs with any intention of the mind, even an inconspicuous one; such that, every welcoming smile, or every slight of the eyes, will impinge the Self as much as it affects the Other; slowly and gradually transforming the Self accordingly. To this extent, every intention will affect the actor with an intensity relative to the moral weight of the transgression; so that, analogous to the legal system, small infractions will have minor repercussions for the actor—which may be easily compensated—whereas significant violations, like a felony, will provoke protracted and severe psychological complications. Moreover, the repercussions on the actor are irrespective of the effect on the victim: as it is the intention and action which affects one's mind.

Although one thoughtless gossip, for example, will have little effect on your psychological well-being, pernicious gossiping will gradually consolidate into an envious personality which despises oneself as much as others. If you are the type of person that is often critical of others, then over time your mind will grow heavy with negativity, with increasing anger, and insecurity. If you are hateful, then you will grow bitter with Self-hatred. If you cheat or steal from others, then you will never be satisfied, you will always be lacking, always hungry for more. If you engross your mind with lust, then you will never be at peace. And so, on and on, the salt we throw at others is from our own increasing store.

While the maxim "do unto others as you would have done unto you" may impinge on the conscience, its effect is either from a sophistical fear of fate, or a concern for some future celestial judgement, or out of intellectual righteousness, without any perceived immediate or direct effect on the actor; in other words, you can always entertain the possibility that you might get away with it. However, now we know that there is more. For, since consciousness is essentially not anything, then every intention is in essence a becoming: the grasping of evil makes us evil, and the grasping of good makes us good. In conclusion, due to the nature of our Nothingness, the human universe is necessarily moral, as I cannot hurt others without hurting myself first: *I do unto myself as I do unto others.*

The Problem with Happiness

We all want to be happy. Even with the most perverse offense, the distorted mind is seeking what it believes will bring happiness. A suicidal person believes death will finally bring happiness. Many of us determine the value of our relationships according to how much satisfaction it affords Me—the "my way or the highway" approach. Happiness is even guaranteed in the U.S. Constitution.

Our desire for happiness drives much of the economy. The makers of perfumes, beauty and health products, and clothing all spend a lot of money trying to convince us that a better physical appearance will bring more happiness to our lives. We have restaurants, movies, television, video games, cell phones, all kinds of fun foods and ice creams, sport cars, vacations, pets, nightclubs and happy hour, just to mention a few of the many things which bring cheerfulness and pleasantness to our lives. With so many available options for happiness, it is hard to believe that there could be unhappy people around. Nonetheless, the overabundance of entertainment is more indicative of our dissatisfaction and boredom than of self-fulfillment.

While most people could come up with a quick list of the things which would make them happy, philosophers and psychologists have been for ages scratching their heads trying to figure out what exactly happiness is, without much agreement or success. Generally defined as a state of wellbeing (like defining water as something liquid), the latest research concludes that the ability to be happy is basically genetically determined (Seligman 2002)—just a little depressing if you ask me—although a happiness gene has not been discovered yet, and there seems to be more to being happy than just feeling good.

So, if we can't really define what happiness is, maybe it's just.................not suffering?

Under the heading of "suffering," we can list the many things which we don't like. We can start with vegetables—oh, if they tasted like cookies, what happiness! Then there is homework, tests, book reports, entrance exams: our education is full of stresses and unpleasantness, and it seems like it never ends. Some people enjoy exercise, but I find that laying on a couch watching a movie or taking a nap is a lot more pleasant. Although for most people work is not a terrible thing, we don't call it entertainment, and few people are ever looking forward to Monday. Therefore, it appears that in life we must suffer many unpleasant things, but it is clear that if we follow only our sense of gratification, we will end up not so well: unhealthy, illiterate, and unemployed. As we have seen, suffering is what shapes us, what identifies us, and what builds character.

So apparently the line between happiness and suffering is a bit blurry: since we also need suffering to be happy. This is indeed true when it comes to marriage. With the prospect of uncomplicated physical pleasure, reliable company, and happiness ever after, almost everyone wants to get married. However, the fantasy of the wedding quickly gives way to the reality of two individuals cohabitating with different interests and expectations. There are misunderstandings, there are power struggles, there are fears of losing oneself or one another, there is suffering; there is reconciliation, intense pleasures, distrust, and more suffering; and if both are brave enough and sincere enough to get through all the conflicts without divorce, then there is a deepening of the relationship, and a deeper understanding of each other and of life—with divorce, a deep sorrow, a sense of personal loss, confusion, and a starting all over again. In general, married people live longer, are healthier, are more content, and are less likely to commit suicide than single persons. However, suicide is highest among divorcees, and the risk of divorce is nearly 50%! So, are married persons really happier? Well, that all depends on how we define happiness—but it does seem to be a risky gamble.

Since it is difficult to decide what happiness is, maybe we can determine what it is not.

Even though most everyone would agree that material wealth by itself cannot buy happiness, it may not be so obvious why this is so. First, because the pleasure from material things is short lasting, and although a "reset" of desire might seem a good thing—as the prospect for endless enjoyment of potato chips—unbridled indulgence leads instead to addiction or boredom, due to the saturation of the pleasure receptors. Take chocolate, for example, you might love it occasionally, but eat it for breakfast, lunch, and dinner and after one day you will hate it. That new purse looks very attractive on the store shelf, but once it's yours it does not look as flashy as that other one on the shelf, and after a while the closet is full of purses—and shoes. The same goes for the new house, the new car, the boat: once it is yours, it quickly loses its glamour. It is the saturation (the habituation) of the receptors of pleasure which also drives drug and alcohol addicts to keep increasing the dose in order to get their high. It has been this capacity to become habituated to almost any situation, which allowed humanity to thrive in the most inhospitable of circumstances, which also limits the extent to which we can experience pleasure.

The other reason the world cannot satisfy us is that it is foreign to our nature: we experience only a conscious reflection (the phenomenon) of the world, not the world itself. If you attend carefully to sensual experience you will notice that you can never quite get at it, it is always at a little distance away: you can never truly, *directly*, experience the world. You taste the chocolate ice cream, but the experience is always fleeting, never wholly real, so you keep licking away until it is all gone, never feeling truly satisfied, just feeling full. As a result, the things of the world can bring about only a sense of pleasure, briefly, but not happiness.

Relationships are more satisfying than material things, and more interesting, primarily because there is more variety involved. During intimate interaction, minds resonate with one another in a mutual feedback of acknowledgment which make social interaction fascinating —a kind of mind-merging. Scientists have found increased levels of oxytocin, a hormone released by the penial gland of the brain, to be associated with happy relationships and social bonding. The more intimate two people become, the stronger the psychological bonds which develop, and the more satisfying the interaction. Unfortunately, as previously discussed with marriage, relationships are complicated and frustrating, and oxytocin levels cannot stay high indefinitely. As a result, although life is more interesting, and more dramatic, when shared with a significant other, it cannot be relied on as a stable source of happiness.

A successful career and personal accomplishments can be a great source of self-fulfillment and satisfaction, but also precarious. Like material things, after some time our accomplishments and interests also lose their luster. Often the chase proves more exciting than the reward, so that many become disillusioned after attaining a long sought-after success—especially if the reward is in the form of unfulfilling material wealth. It is a little shocking, and disheartening, to see the aged movie stars, musicians, and athletes, who so inspired us when we were young with their power and charm, now worn and wrinkled, still trying to hold on to the past. Making an honest living and raising a good family affords great personal satisfaction and foments much happiness, but like any other relationship, it is full of struggles; later the kids grow away, memories fade, and the photos are a bittersweet reminder of what has been lost. A successful career can be a great ego booster, but there is always the looming possibility of job loss, the constant sacrifice of personal and family time, and the unavoidable irony of retirement. Although intellectual pursuits significantly expand the breadth and depth of one's personality, which is conducive to maturing and emotional stability, one eventually comes to the realization that there are more questions than answers, more Nothingness than gratification. It is because all these forms of personal satisfaction hinge on a continuously changing world, that they cannot secure and sustain an enduring happiness.

Aristotle realized about 2350 years ago that the virtuous life was the means to the ultimate happiness of Eudaimonia (more or less the satisfaction of having a good spirit). Virtue, he observed, is instructed by adhering to moderation, or the Golden Mean, and by exercising integrity, courage, honesty, and good citizenship. At around the same period, and across a continent, Gautama the Buddha was teaching the Not-self doctrine and the Four Noble Truths as the middle way to the ultimate happiness of Nibbana. These brilliant men discovered that what can be called true happiness, or contentment, can only come from the peace of mind afforded by the wisdom which arises from the practice of virtue and contemplation: from being a good person and from knowing your mind.

The problem with happiness is that it is not an "objective" thing, it is not something you will find in the world. As soon as I start to *think* of what it is that will *make me* happy then I am positing it out in the World, a World which is impermanent, and subsequently, dissatisfying and stressful. Whether it is an object, a per-

51

son, an idea, a belief, or anything which I attempt to reach for outside of my Being, it will be something foreign to me, and ultimately disappointing.

True happiness cannot come from that which is of the World, but rather from that which is unchanging, that is, from our Being. How we get to this happy state of Being is what the Water is all about.

II

The Water

The Personal Universe

As we have seen thus far, it is easier to speak of what we are not, than to know who we are. Categorically, anything that exists as an object of our awareness, *that* we are not. We cannot know what we are because we are the ones looking: We are an absolute subjectivity which cannot take itself as an object of awareness: in the same manner that an eye cannot see itself seeing. And yet, the only thing which we can truly know is that we are: We know that there is someone looking!

We have seen that the body belongs more to the earth than to us. We can observe our thoughts and emotions as they appear and disappear from our awareness, and therefore we can verify that we are not the thoughts or emotions, any more than a song we sing, or a stomachache we suffer.

We know that we are conscious; but what is consciousness?

Consciousness cannot be defined without being circular. Typically defined as "the state of being aware," it is again like saying that water is something which is liquid. The reason for this is that consciousness, or awareness, is not like anything else: it is not made of anything, and there is nothing to compare it to. Consciousness manifests in living beings as an essence, as a presence which overwhelms the physical framework. Yet, while animals exhibit varying degrees of consciousness, only the human being comports with awareness of awareness, with an awareness of self-existence. Awareness of awareness should not be construed as self-awareness: as in awareness of Self. Awareness of Self is a rational, thinking, comprehension of the Self as an object of consciousness. Rather, by awareness of awareness, we signify that pre-reflective consciousness by which I ascertain my existence in the act of existing. This certainty of self-existence, this particular human way of being conscious, we designate as Being. Human consciousness manifests as Being. This Being, this existing, is not something which exists *for me*, as does emotion or a discomfort, as a noun, but rather as the present participle of the verb to be. Being is what I am, and it is something of which I have no doubts about.

As Being, human consciousness is at the same time what is most obvious, and what is most mysterious.

Human consciousness, as Being, is what is most obvious because it is where everything "is". The general impression is that we have a consciousness which resides in the brain, which is in the body, which is in the world, but in reality, it is the other way around. The world and the body exist in consciousness. That is because everything that exists, exists as a conscious experience for someone. The color red which I see, for example, is the result of a light wave which affects the nerves of the visual pathway to produce a neural configuration of red in my brain; it exists in a manner just for me. In other words, no one knows what red is outside of an individual conscious experience of red; and the same goes for all the other sense impressions, which is the entire known universe. Our true apprehension of the world is not as if we were looking through a window at something out there outside our heads, or as if watching a movie on a screen. The universe is specifically "projected," or reconstructed, in the brain, and we apprehend it as a

56

conscious experience. In other words, *the World, as we know it, is made out of consciousness*. What exists outside of our awareness of it, we cannot ever know. We can investigate this reality again, as described previously, by pressing on the eyelid of an open eye while keeping the other closed; that you can move the image with the finger is possible because it is a conscious object of the mind. The reason that we manage the world effectively, despite not experiencing it directly, is because consciousness represents it very accurately, and we all have the same way of being conscious. It is because everything in *my* universe is made of *my* consciousness that it is so challenging to identify my Being.

Human consciousness is the most mysterious thing. Despite the best efforts of science, it cannot be found from where in the brain, or how, consciousness arises. Consciousness does not arise in any particular structure of the brain, instead, it seems to be everywhere and nowhere, yet operating the brain centers (like the speech, auditory, visual, motor areas, and the frontal cortex), and compensating the deficiency of one with the over development of another. The brain appears more as an instrument of the awareness: functioning much like a computer, organizing and filtering information, and with programming capabilities. For example, researchers have been able to measure that the retina sends about 10 million bits of data per second to the brain (U. Penn. 2006), but we can only consciously handle about 60 bits per second (MIT 2009); that means that all those millions of bits have been organized by the visual cortex into a comprehensive structure prior to conscious perception. Thus, when looking at a painting by Jackson Pollock, we can see the big picture even though the visual system is receiving millions of details almost all at once. Similarly, we train and practice an activity to program the brain to function much faster than we can be continuously conscious of, as when reading or playing the piano. Therefore, the brain is like a machine, and the awareness, or the pre-reflective consciousness, is the mysterious machine opera-tor. Although we appear to be aware of many things all at once, conscious attention is singular; that is, we can only attend to one unit-thing at a time. Which means that even though it appears that we can see and listen at the same time, in reality, conscious atten-tion is switching back and forth so quickly that it gives the impres-sion to be happening simultaneously. It is also the reason you can-not focus on a portion of a picture and be aware of the whole at once. Furthermore, because awareness always occupies a perspec-tive outside of a succession of entities, it must be unitary and time-less; otherwise it would have to change with the series and could not be aware of it. But even more significantly, it is consciousness which gives everything that sense of being real, of existing: What makes the machine come alive!

All cosmological evidence points to an evolving universe. While the material universe is cooling down by expanding and exploding, that is, by increasing entropy, living beings move in the opposite direction, decreasing entropy by creating ever greater organization and complexity. All life forms on earth demonstrate an unrelenting urge to grow, flourish, and evolve, which seems unstoppable. There is strong evidence that living organisms have survived 5 mass ex-tinctions, wiping out 80-95% of creatures per event, to again thrive with breathtaking diversity. The theory of evolution describes how this life energy is organized through the interaction with the envi-ronment in developing increasingly complex organisms; and with increased complexity, we observe a clearer expression of con-sciousness. With the higher animals and primates, we recognize a more evolved awareness evidenced by markedly elaborate behav-iors. With humans, however, consummate neural complexity en-gendered a transformative change in consciousness, manifesting with the expression of self-awareness and creativity. This radical change in awareness enabled a conscious experience of the world at a distance (as from a point of view apart from the world), that made possible a mental representation of objects and ideas—releasing the mind to take off like a jet plane with inventiveness. Something happened to a pre-human primate (homo sapiens) about 200,000 years ago which freed its consciousness from its cohesion to the world, a nihilation of the world from consciousness, which left a Nothingness in its aftermath. This freedom was the birth of the individual Being: the personal universe.

Although there is conclusive evidence that a human being is a primate, evolved from a primitive ape, and before that from a long line of small tree-dwelling animals, the difference from the great apes to humans is so great that it defies simple lineage—it is like saying that the jet plane is a direct descendant of the bicycle because they both have wheels. The transformation was more in accord with a quantum change of state, as when water changes to steam. Indeed, when considering all the wondrous accomplishments of humans—in science, technology, engineering, and the arts—it is quite ludicrous to see ourselves as intelligent apes. A Beethoven symphony gives evidence enough of this transcendent nature of the human intellect: the profound and complex aesthetic expression of the passion and mystery of human existence.

Truly, when considering the profound complexity and astounding creativity of the human intellect, it is difficult to concede that it is the outcome of an alchemy of non-conscious material and the fallout of some blind urge for survival. Human intelligence and creativity far exceed what is necessary for survival on earth—in this the simple cockroach has been by far more successful than us. Although it is evident that the evolutionary pressure generated by the clash of intelligent beings would foment increasing intelligence, it is open to speculation as to how *self*-consciousness would secure an evolutionary advantage, as its intention is directed towards the survival of the Self—with fear and trembling—rather than the group. In other words, it would be more plausible that humans would have evolved into something akin to intelligent (un-self-conscious) belligerent ants; where the individual would be unimportant, easily expendable, and fearless. What all our scientific, artistic, and religious pursuits indicate is that human Being transcends consciousness towards an *individuality*.

But is our individuality just an illusion of consciousness? Is our experience of existing and of self-consciousness just another gimmick of nature? Or are we parts of some larger being—perhaps a universal consciousness manifesting with an illusion of individuality? Is all this eating and drinking, working, striving, learning, reproducing, fighting, praying, crying, and then dying, all for nothing—all just some kind of existential practical joke?

No, the drama and suffering of human existence can only be fathomable and justifiable as a process of individuation of conscious beings, as a personification of consciousness; any other inference would be fraught with absurdity. Here, the questioning of existence and the dread of dying is already evidence of a transcendence of materiality towards a singularity of Being.

Although in our daily routines we behave as if we are a mind in a body, in a neighborhood, in a city, standing on earth and looking up at the sky, the reality is the other way around: the heavens, the earth, the neighborhood, the body, all that we have ever invented and discovered, and all that has ever been known to exist, exist in individual minds. Everything which each one of us experiences exists in a personal universe. Although it seems otherwise, there is nothing which can be said to exist outside individual awareness; there is no way of knowing it or even thinking about it (as any thought would again be within our frame of consciousness).

The importance of this insight is that the center of the universe is shifted to the individual: to each person as a singularity of existence. Now, I no longer see myself from without, as an object among objects, or an object for others, but as an absolute subjectivity, at the center of a restless universe. No longer are others just people, just population, the proletariat, bourgeois, a class, a race, a number, but many individual universes; each with an intimate life, a fear of death, and deserving of acknowledgment, respect, peace, and happiness.

Furthermore, my universe is now my responsibility and my contingency, one which I can enrich with love, kindness, peaceful-ness, integrity, and meaningfulness; or pollute with anger, hatred, jealousy, slander, and hostility. My universe will become what I bring into it.

As I sit with eyes closed and focus my attention on the entirety of my experience, I discover the following:

As I listen to a sound, it exists as if out in the world, at some distance from the center of my Being. My breathing, the stretching of the abdomen, the sensations of my body, of my skin, these feel a little closer, but still, as something at a slight distance from my point of view. A thought occurs in my field of awareness, a little closer even, but still as something separate that I am as-looking-at. When I attempt to experience who I am, however, there is nothing: here I have no extension in space, no awareness of changing. I can-not tell whether my consciousness is male or female, young or old, tall or short. From this point of view, all that reflects my existing I find at a distance from me, as an object for me, and not who I am; the body, the senses, the emotions, ideas, are all something that I am looking at. It is in this sense that there is no self, no person, or thing, which is Me, no entity which I can point to as an objective permanent me; everything is Not-self for me. The permanent me, the only unchanging me, I cannot describe. I do not exist as any-thing, for I am the center of all existing things: I AM at the center of my known universe. And yet, if there is anything that I am une-quivocally sure of, as that which is most real to me, it is that I exist. This is Being: an actuality, an immediacy, a singularity, a Nothing-ness. Here, my relationship to the World is through the Nothing, as a "nihilation" of all beings away from my centeredness in Being.

At the center of human being, Being and Nothingness become singular, and manifest an absolute Freedom.

Perhaps you have heard that each mind is a universe, but this is generally stated to mean that each person has preferences or tastes. Now we see that it is literally true, that each human being is the center of an incomparable conscious universe; each of us with free will—and an existential problem. This material universe is the means by which a human consciousness becomes aware of itself. Like a womb, the universe gives birth to Being.

Being a Good Person

At the very least, to be happy, to be content, to have peace of mind, you must be a good person. Your universe, in whichever way you wish to found it—whether your faith rests in God, religion, evolution, or just yourself—is intrinsically moral.

The study of ethical behavior with its social and legal implications has filled volumes and preoccupied the best philosophical minds. However, technically it all boils down to one simple tenet: "do unto others as you would have them do unto you." This Golden Rule is dictated by a conscience founded on the knowledge and understanding of what is right and wrong. Embedded in this moral principle is the ethical mandate to respect the dignity and essential human rights of one another: the right to life, freedom, and the pursuit of happiness.

We make moral judgments in accordance with values and beliefs we have garnered from our ancestry and culture, from our formal and informal education, and from our good and bad fortune, with the intent of achieving some personal benefit. We make ethical decisions with respect to the established laws of the society we live in. For most of us, our moral decisions are reflexive and preconditioned by our past experiences, emotions, and a particular present situation; rarely are judgments made after careful reflection with regards to unwavering moral principles. As for example, after a good night sleep and a good breakfast one may shrug off a slow driver on the way to work; but following a long day of labor and hungry, the same person may instead react with road rage in the same situation. Not unusually, someone may be kind and helpful with coworkers yet abusive with the family, or vice versa.

What we consider the good or benefit of our actions is as well conditioned by what is socio-culturally reproachable or commendable. Specifically, the legal system is generally founded on rules which help people get along with each other within culturally defined norms. As a result, we ordinarily make moral assessments and hold ethical standards with concern for the social consequences of our behavior. Even the guilt we feel from breaking the Golden Rule is mostly due to a fear of reproach from an internalized Other. However, there could be a situation where a moral transgression and its subsequent harm would be unbeknownst and inconsequential to the victim, for example: an elderly person gives a lottery ticket to a gasoline station attendant for scanning; the attendant gets it confused with another ticket on the counter which scans with no value; after the customer leaves, the attendant realizes his error and scans the other ticket which turns out to have a winning of $1000; as he looks out the window, he sees the customer pumping gas into his Mercedes and remembers his rent is past due. Now, it appears that the attendant could keep the winnings without doing any harm to the customer—who seems not to be hurting for money. The attendant may not experience guilt from keeping the winnings since he has an urgent necessity, the action was not done with malice, and the customer will not be aware of being a victim. While some may condemn this action as stealing, few would realize that the real victim in this situation is the attendant.

Rarely are we mindful of the impact our moral decisions have on our own Self. Breaking the Golden Rule has more than just extraneous repercussions, as something from which you can distance yourself or willingly remain unaffected, because, as we discovered earlier, the mind is a Nothingness, and therefore, every action is in effect a projection of an internal state; meaning that we effectively become what we wish or do onto others. We had called this the Moral Red Rule, that "you do unto yourself what you do, or intend, unto others." It is the disregard for the Red Rule which little by little, day by day, conditions what will be our ultimate state of unhappiness—our contingency of salt. From this we can see that not only do the major moral transgressions generate severe internal noxious states—such as a quenchless state of lacking from being a thief, or the neurosis and depression resulting from committing murder or sexual abuse—but even seemingly inconsequential transgression, such as envy or gossiping, or even a slight of the eyes—or even the thought of it—will over time dull and stain to some extent the wholesomeness and dignity of the Self. This psychological repercussion is what constitutes the true workings of what is called Karma (Kamma in Pali), as expounded by the Buddha in the profound Paticca-Samuppada Sutta (the Dependent Origination Sutta), and not the superstitious belief in some abstruse cosmic justice parceling out rebirths (such as, for example, that if one dies a glutton they will be reborn a swine, or if you are good you will be reborn beautiful, etc.). This moral contingency is innate of the human mind, and it is therefore universal. Thence, heedlessly, we create our heaven and hell in our minds, here on earth.

Our moral disposition is contingent on the Self which we sustain and endeavor to protect. On one extreme of the moral spectrum is the egocentric individual whose absolute identification with the Self obscures any comprehension or interest in the wellbeing of others. This is a Machiavellian Self: the bully, the compulsive liar, the tyrant, the abuser, the serial killer. Having no interest or respect for the Look of the Other, this person does not experience any guilt; the Others exists only as convenient objects—there is no mystery behind their eyes. The selfish person sees the world through the demands of their Self, others are mere instruments. This is a tragic person who moves oblivious to the personal repercussions of his/her actions, inadvertently scheming their own affliction and undoing.

On the other end of the moral spectrum is the saint, as one who has attained moral perfection such that all ethical decisions and intentions are informed only by the clear understanding of what is beneficial for the wellbeing of others. This person has transcended all reference to a Self as a source of motivation; the ego exists only as a transparent convention useful for interacting with others. This person is her/his own end, having nothing to gain or to lose from the World or others, with nothing to become. Her/his happiness emanates spontaneously from the essence of just existing. The saint comports with total freedom, confidence, and integrity; with a kindness which issues from wholesomeness rather than sentimentality; with a demeanor distinguished by impeccable transparency and authenticity.

Most of us find ourselves between these extremes, stumbling between Self-directed intentions and sentimental sympathy, motivated more by emotions than ideals. While religions generally stress the importance of kindness, respect, forgiveness, and charity as requisites for spiritual and personal growth, these are largely endorsed as counsel rather than imperatives. However, if we are mindful of our thoughts and emotions, and observant of the personal repercussions of our actions, then we can avoid heedless wrongdoing and unintentional harm to ourselves and others. *This is the true categorical imperative: that we must be kind to others, as a condition to our own happiness and sanity of mind.*

Because of the subject-object structure of our interactions, we are always obligated to react in some manner to the presence of an-

Other—even no reaction would still be a reaction. In the meeting of two minds, there is always an acknowledgment, always a communication to one another, and always a psychological consequence to each other. We know how it feels when we are greeted with a smile and kind words; it livens our mood, and we are predisposed to the same for others further on. We also know how someone's disdain or cold-shoulder can be disconcerting and provoke us to a similar reaction, or at least discourage us from showing kindness to others.

The alternatives for reacting, regardless of any conditioning factors, quickly become discernable in the mind, which we can consider in our encounter with an-Other. However, most of us react reflexively and emotionally with little consideration for the repercussions our actions have on ourselves and others. Like the smoker, who rationalizing that "you have to die of something" is ignorant or dismissive of the misery of living with COPD, the agony of dying from lung cancer, and the emotional pain caused to loved ones, rarely do we worry about the grave and unfathomable consequences our actions have on our Self and others, how each thoughtless act contributes to the collective of apathy, hatred, prejudice, and abusiveness. On the other hand, if we mindfully consider our reactions, preferring always to be kind, considerate, and understanding of others, always careful not to cause undue suffering, then we contribute to the wellbeing and happiness of others, ourselves, and society in general

To cause suffering is not per se unwholesome, and it is sometimes a moral obligation. For example, a parent will cause distress to a child when appropriately punishing to prevent future harm and greater suffering—such as from refusing to wear a seat belt or not wanting to do homework—in this case, not punishing would be the unwholesome act. As well, we cause suffering with medical procedures and the enforcement of rules and laws, but the consequences of avoiding these would be generally disastrous. As we discussed previously, suffering is part of our human condition and necessary for our healthy development. A good person, therefore, acts with a clear understanding of what is benevolent and beneficial.

We all share an intuitive apprehension of each other's feelings, emotions, fears, suffering, and joys, because we all share the same way of being conscious, and because we grow up with each Other. Despite cultural differences and different life experiences, which may affect our expression of empathy, all rational beings have an appreciation of another's desire for freedom, respect, and happiness. This is what informs our moral behavior: that we know how others suffer.

However, you do not become a virtuous person simply by abstaining from doing harm—as you are not adding salt to your glass, but not water either. As we learn from the saints, it is by helping and being kind to others that you help yourself—by adding water. In effect, becoming a good person is coincidental with the releasing of the Self, by being un-self-ish, because the essence of the pure human consciousness is benevolent; it is saintly. The Buddha expressed the importance of this realization in his Metta Sutta:

This is what should be done
By one who is skilled in goodness,
And who knows the path of peace: Let them be able and upright,
Straightforward and gentle in speech,
Humble and not conceited,
Contented and easily satisfied,
Unburdened with duties and frugal in their ways.
Peaceful and calm and wise and skillful,
Not proud or demanding in nature.
Let them not do the slightest thing
That the wise would later reprove.
Wishing: In gladness and in safety,

May all beings be at ease...
Let none deceive another,
Or despise any being in any state.
Let none through anger or ill-will
Wish harm upon another.
Even as a mother protects with her life
Her child, her only child,
So with a boundless heart
Should one cherish all living beings;
Radiating kindness over the entire world...
Freed from hatred and ill-will
(Amaravati 2013)

By not causing harm to others we avoid adding salt to our store; by being kind and helpful, we add more water. Every encounter with another person creates a situation whereby an attitude will need to be taken and a decision made as to how to interact; that is, with every personal encounter we are obliged to add a drop of water or a grain of salt to our glass. From this perspective, it would seem more conducive to peace of mind if one could live alone, but then there would not be much personal growth. It is the interaction with one another which discloses our deepest moral shortcomings, our hidden emotional wounds, our suppressed prejudices, and our greatest fears: which reveals the Self.

A strong commitment to be a good person will promote the peace of mind which facilitates further mental hygiene. When we hold wholesome thoughts in mind and act with kindness to others, then these immediately condition our own pleasantness and happiness; if we are hurtful to ourselves and others, then the mind will immediately become uncomfortable and unhappy.

Any concern with one's role in a damaging situation should be corrected as best and as soon as possible; then, one must sincerely commit to avoiding further transgressions. Any attempt at rationalization, denial, or suppression, will only succeed in adding more salt to the wounds of the Self.

The moral health of our personal universe is ultimately contingent on our attachment to the World as Self. All unhappiness, all hurtful actions, all evil, all sins, are the result of grasping the Self in ignorance of what constitutes true happiness. When being selfish and greedy, we are reacting to a sense of lacking, to insecurity, to a fear of loss of Self. When we are jealous, angry, hurtful, or prejudiced, we are reacting with aggression out fear of injury to our Self. The more tightly we grasp at a Selfish World, the more fearful we become, the more hurtful we grow, the more harm we cause to ourselves and others, and the greater the suffering we will have to endure. There are no happy villains.

When we are uncritical of others, we learn to accept of our own imperfections. When we are kind to others, we add to our own peace and contentment. With every "good morning," every smile, every word of encouragement, every word of praise, every seemingly unimportant gesture of goodwill, we water the seeds of kindness in the hearts of others. When we teach our children to be tolerant, respectful, helpful, and kind to others, we plant seeds of love in their hearts which will last a lifetime. When we respond to aggression with understanding, fairness, and composure, we heal our old wounds and add to the happiness and the peace of the world.

Truly, if there is any substantial meaning that is allotted to human existence, it must rest on a moral universe, on being a good person; because nothing of value can be extracted from a world which is through and through Not-self.

Being with Others

Being with others is never easy. Yet it is much more difficult if both are working from the ignorance of Self. It is impossible for two persons to get along if both are drowning in their salty water: you must first learn to swim well yourself to help others swim along.

Therefore, the problem with others starts with me. If I believe that I am a particular person, a Self, then I am pressed to protect this Self from the threats of others, I am vulnerable, I am fearful. First, because I am never quite sure who this Self is that I am protecting—cannot ever get a good grip on it because I can never create a permanent object of Me for myself—and second, because the only objective perspective which I am granted of my Self comes from Others. If you value yourself as a successful businessperson, then your self-worth rests on the approval and opinions of your clients or coworkers. If you define yourself as a writer, then you are as good as your book sales. A mother and a father are vulnerable to the relationship with their children. From the perspective of Self, your happiness or sadness will depend on what others give you. If, on the other hand, you can release the World as not who you are, as not your true self, then you can attain veritable freedom from others. When you are free of the Self, then there is nothing to protect, and nothing risked: you become transparent to the opinions of others.

But others can be difficult. The worldly Others are not only a mystery to me but to themselves as well. In the Other, as Sartre explains, we perceive both an objectivity and a subjectivity: a subjectivity that is trying to be an object for itself. The Other is searching for acknowledgment and approval as an object-for-itself, and at the same time in fear of dis-integrating as subject-for-itself. As a responsible Other to an-Other person, we must reflect on what is most beneficial—whether acceptance, understanding, kindness, approval, or disapproval—with the clear understanding that a person who is not Self-afflicted would be at peace and would not be hurtful. For One who has transcended their Self, the aggressions from others are transpersonal, and as a result, bearable and manageable despite being unpleasant —more like a stomachache. It is in this context where we can bear the pain and "turn the other cheek."

When the Other is a family member or a close friend, the aggression, the depression, the indifference, the rejection, will provoke stronger emotions and feelings of empathy and sympathy: a suffering with, a sadness for. We cannot take on, as much as we would want to, the consequences and misfortunes of the wrong decisions and actions that others have wrought upon themselves: there is only so much we can do to relieve the physical or the mental suffering of others. At a certain point we must exercise composure, *equanimity*, with the understanding that each one of us has a personal road of self-realization to travel, and ultimately, as we have seen, suffering is instrumental in our formation and maturing.

The comprehension that the injurious behaviors of others proceed from the fear brought about by their attachment to the Self, and that each one of us is constrained to a unique path of self-realization, opens the way for a peace of mind which can allow for forgiveness. Forgiveness thereof consoles the Other, as it dissolves our own limitations.

We have discovered the absolute Freedom of Being, but this freedom is an attribute of an unconditioned consciousness; it should not be misconstrued to vindicate a disregard for social conventions and responsibilities or to undermine the respect for the sensibilities of others. Uninhibited or immoral behavior instead confines us, for it reinforces attachment to a corrupt, ungoverned Self which becomes increasingly defective and impulsive. Existential Freedom liberates us from identification with any one mode of behavior or a desire for anything or anyone; as a result, we become free to accept conformity—which means that we don't have to prove anything. We cannot avoid the moral responsibility to care for ourselves and for others, if we want to arrive at true freedom.

Caring for ourselves and others entails respect and prudence with our bodies and that of others. Although the body is Not-self, not our true essence, it is nonetheless our means of becoming individuals, of existing in time, and of relating to each other. We should eat healthy, exercise regularly, practice good hygiene, and help others to do the same. In practicing modesty towards ourselves and others, we transcendent our animal natures towards a supramundane dignity. Provoking our animal instincts instead serves to degrade our humanity, binding us further to the earth. Often, however, restraint becomes difficult due to the powerful influence sexual attraction has on our psyche. So, to reach a balance, to train in moderation, the Buddhists apply a technique called *Asubha* which consists in directing attention to the unattractive aspects of the body, such as the bodily secretions, body odors and fluids, and the various characteristics of the intestinal tract—to all those natural aspects of the body which we work so hard to suppress, disguise, or decorate. Even the beautiful attributes of the body are not so pleasant from a different perspective. For example, you may love your hair, but it can be pretty repulsive to find it in your soup. Or, take the most beautiful photo of a face which you can find, look at it upside-down for a minute, and you will see how unattractive the same facial features now become. Asubha is a method for developing control of the desire for the body, not to produce disgust towards it—that is, don't do this too much. Realistically, the body is neither beautiful nor ugly, these are just cultural and psychological values we project on to it. We do a lot of projecting on each other, and it dramatically conditions our salt production.

Sometimes we become frustrated when we are kind to others, when we do good things to help other people, but in return we receive contempt, jealousy, or exploitation. Sometimes we see others profiting from their abuses and lies, while we struggle to make an honest living. While we strive to do good, to add water to our glass, others are pouring salt into theirs and looking none the worse for it, or even happier. Therefore, you may wonder, if the universe is intrinsically moral, then why do bad things happen to good people, and vice versa?

It all has to do with Freedom. If our minds were not free, then we would not be capable of evil, but then we would not be self-conscious, and our behavior would be limited to biological needs—the reason why animals do not murder. But because we are free of the World, we become the victims of our unrestrained, ignorant desires. To the extent that there are no natural boundaries to the internal motivations and behaviors of humans, we need laws and punishment as deterrents—and still despite, there are many who transgress these, causing irredeemable harm to good people. Alas, this is the price we pay for our self-consciousness and free will: It is the knowledge of good and evil which makes us capable of sin. And yes! good things always come to good people, and vice versa, but not in the manner by which most persons consider their happiness, rather from the peace of mind and contentment which is inherent of an unsullied conscience.

The Other is always a mystery. Sometimes we learn of persons who seem naturally evil, excessively cruel and insensitive, and then discover the abuse and suffering they had to endure as a child that drove them to be so. But even our closest Others—spouse, parents, children, siblings—surprise us with unexpected reactions, choices, and behaviors. Ultimately, it is best to understand that each one of us has a personal road to travel, and instead of condemning, to have sympathy for the suffering each of us will eventually have endure from the consequences of inappropriate actions and misfortunes. Each one of us is burdened to learn from our mistakes or continue to suffer until we do—that's the Red Rule.

Each and every one of us has an ethical mandate towards others who impinge upon our universe: who come into our lives. The reciprocal response in that encounter will be a determinant in the wellbeing for one another. The smile we give, the attention rendered, and the respect we show will be a healing touch which will inspire others to do the same further on. It is difficult to fathom what positive reverberations we may have launched with a single word or act of kindness, or how we may have inadvertently precipitated some tragedy with our indifference or animosity.

Our wholesome response to each other is through love. But what is love?

Love is a word we use in innumerable occasions in reference to numerous things, and nonetheless, we all seem to understand exactly what we mean. However, we shouldn't *love* our spouse the same way we *love* pizza or a good perfume. Love is often used to indicate we like something very much for our own selfish pleasure—like eating pizza—or to have a desire for something without being physically intimate, as in "I love to play the piano," or "I would love to get together for lunch." We make love and fall in love, which should mean two different things. The love we have for our children is not the same love we feel for a spouse, and not the love we profess in religion. But what I find in common to many kinds of "loves" is that they all relate to Me: they all in one way or another have to do with My needs.

Much of our music, movie, and television entertainment involves the drama and excitement of sexual or romantic love. As we have discussed, sexual attraction and the sex drive are forces of nature which affect us through the body. As a power of creation, it all has to do with Me as a body, that is, for the pleasure which I receive in the transmission of my genes: as an intention, it is most profoundly selfish. In a genuine loving relationship, however, the meaning of sex is essentially transformed. In this, it becomes the consummate means of being intimate, the closest we can be with another person, and it becomes most wonderfully human when the unselfish pleasure we give is returned with the same intention. Across the body, we can express our most profound devotion and care for another person; we can reveal how completely we cherish our lover. Animals are not sexually intimate, they are as naïve in their mating as they are in their aggression—for them, it is all nature. A loving relationship, grounded in mutual respect, trust, profound affection, and selfless sexual passion, entirely transcends the Self: it is rooted in the divine nature of humanity: it attains authentic intimacy.

However, for the love which engenders perfect peace of mind, which transcends the World as Not-self, we can ascribe to the word *Agape*. Originating from the Greco-Christian tradition in conveying the love of God for mankind, it means to cherish and appreciate beings for their own sake. It is a love with no Self-reference; it is Self-less; it emanates from the very essence of Being. The Buddhists name this manifestation of unselfish love the Brahma-viharas (or divine attributes), which consists of four qualities, namely: loving-kindness, compassion, sympathetic joy, and equanimity.

With Agape, I don't have to like someone to love them: it is not about Me. Rather, our caring for the Other springs forth from an understanding of the contingency of our existence and a profound

appreciation for the Being of others. With Agape, we have the realization that one who is lost to the World-as-Self, is one who is
suffering, is a victim of their destiny (their facticity as per Sartre),
and ignorance, and is worthy of compassion and forgiveness—
"for they know not what they do." (Luke 23:34)

How we develop Agape is through mindfulness. When we encounter someone, we can pay careful attention to the thoughts and
emotions which arise, and our response to them. Depending on
our life experience, our encounter with other persons can trigger a
variety of perceptions, memories, and emotions, which blur our
judgments and condition our reactions and intentions. But with
careful attention, we can observe these prejudices as from a distance and remain in control; then we become empowered to respond with unconditioned acceptance and kindness.

*If you have added much salt to your glass, there is no easy way to remove
it, but you can improve your condition by adding a lot of water; the most immediate and effective way of doing this is by being kind and helpful to others.*

Agape is sympathetic but not sentimental: we understand what
another person is going through, yet we are not moved to act emotionally but rather through benevolence. With Agape, with this
transpersonal love, we do not gain or lose anything when helping
or being kind to others, as there is no motivation which originates
from a Self; instead, our intentions issue from a charitable disposition which arises from the nature of Being.

The universe which matters, the universe which is moral—despite the actions of others—is your personal universe. You draw
the salt or the water that fills your glass, and that will determine the
suffering you will have to bear, and the person you will become.
Yet in being with others: in the end, the water you get is equal to
the water you give.

Being Not-self

With the words "existence precedes essence" Sartre succinctly exposed our predicament. This is the sobering, and perhaps frightening, realization that we are not anything: that we are really nothing. We exist and then are free to make of ourselves as we wish. We are by nature neither good or evil, blessed nor damned, with no original essence, but rather the authors of our values, and the creators of our Self.

If you observe your mind carefully and search for your Self, you will find—as was famously reported by the philosopher David Hume (b.1711, d.1776)—only a succession of thoughts, feelings, emotions, memories, but nothing to which you can point to as yourself, your essence. And yet, who is the one searching?

Our pursuit of happiness is in effect a quest for our true self. We are inspired to become a lawyer, a musician, a businessperson, a politician, a doctor, a spouse, a parent, etc., out of an essential lack of identity, an emptiness, which underlies our innermost being. We have a pre-verbal understanding of our existential unhappiness, as a subtle anguish, which we try to mitigate by grasping the world as Self. We have a longing to find that thing in the World which would thoroughly complete us, that would render us at peace and satisfied.

Our investigation into our true identity has already led us to question our body, the world, our accomplishments, our thoughts, and emotions, and we are compelled to conclude that we are not any of these. Some proclaim, therefore, that the Self is an illusion, and that beyond this fabrication there is nothing, no individual existence. But how can an illusion determine itself an illusion? There would have to be another you looking at yourself being an illusion. The proposition "I am an illusion" is contradictory, as "I am" is a statement of existence; it is like saying "I do not exist."

Therefore, there must be *that* which knows the Self as an illusion, which is not an illusion. But then, how can we know what *that* is, since everything which I can experience is not what I am?

For Sartre, human consciousness is nothing: only as that which is the annihilation of the material world. This consciousness exists only in relation to the world, he says, like a wind which is revealed by the trees, he states:

All at once consciousness is purified, it is clear as a strong wind. There is nothing in it but a movement of fleeing itself, a sliding beyond itself. If, impossible though it may be, you could enter "into" a consciousness, you would be seized by a whirlwind and thrown back outside, in the thick of the dust, near the tree, for consciousness has no "inside." Precisely this being-beyond-itself, this absolute flight, this refusal to be a substance is what makes it be a consciousness. (Intentionality, 1939)

Thus, we have discovered the one who is searching, who is no longer the illusory Self, but now it has been revealed to us as a nothing, an emptiness. Since nothing can come from nothing, Sartre has left it to us to invent ourselves, to create our meaning out of nothing. But is a value which is invented actually valuable? Can we authentically be something we pretend to be? Sartre did not believe so, and even more, felt that all our attempts at authenticity would result in what he called Bad Faith.

Heidegger revealed humankind as Dasein, as the being who has a pre-ontological (or intuitive) understanding of its own existence, and as the One who is the source of the being of all beings. With Dasein, we discover that our Nothingness is at the same time a Being-there (the meaning of Dasein, in German). Being and Nothingness, therefore, become one and the same for the One-who-knows. Yet, as Heidegger proposed, Dasein's being is a *being in time*, so that in the face of death existence is always a problem for Dasein, always an underlying source of anxiety, for in death Dasein returns to nothing.

And so, as it appears, all our projects are ultimately doomed to failure, for we are as strangers in an estranged world: We are thrown in a world not of our making, and then burdened to make ourselves out of nothing! Everywhere we look, everything appears solid except for our own being: our consciousness like a wind, revealed only in the movement of the world, in time. Nothing we can see belongs to us, and everything is negating us!

But maybe we are just looking in the wrong direction.

If we keep trying to discover our true essence through reasoning, through our senses, through our projects, that is, by means of everything which is not of our true nature, then it should not be surprised that we find only a negation of our being-there. We rather need to begin with what never changes for us: our point of view.

If I were to ask you "how do you know you exist," you would be speechless. First, because it is absolutely the most obvious question; and second, because there is no way to prove it! If you answer "I think, therefore I am," or "I breath, therefore I am," the "I am," the existence, already comes first to reveal the thinking, because the *knowing-of* is what reveals the known: it is rather "I am, therefore I think." The only reasonable answer to the question would be tautological: "I know that I exist, because I exist." Or as Sartre says: There is a pre-reflective *cogito* which reveals the *Cartesian cogito*.

What is most obvious is that I exist; and for humans, this pre-reflective certitude of existence is Being.

Being has a "quality" to it, a distinction, a power, a presence; it is what gives everything presence. Alas, words can only *point* to this reality since our "sense of self-existence," our Being, is an absolute subjectivity: it cannot experience itself as an object for itself. However, everything which is known points to the origin of that knowing: to Being. This Being which is not any-thing, is the basis of everything, of the entire World as we know it: *it is where every-thing exists*. The word "Being," nonetheless, is also just another sign which points to this profound experience of existing. A more direct way to this reality is through meditation.

If you sit in a quiet place, with your eyes closed, and start looking for "yourself", eliminating everything which you can experience as an object of knowledge, you will arrive at Being. As all body sensations, emotions, memories, and thoughts fade away, you arrive at the simple state of just existing. In effect, this sense of existing, this Being, is present for you everywhere, all the time, because it is the foundation of reality. The experience of Being is not like a flimsy film or a transparency which covers reality; it is rather an immensely powerful quality which brings everything, the World, into existence, giving everything that sense of being real. That it is difficult to identify is because we are distracted by the manifestations of the World; yet, Being *is* where everything *is*.

Being is an absolute Freedom, and this Freedom is the basis for authenticity. However, as we have seen, this Freedom of Being, for most people, is in potential. This is because as long as there is an attachment to an idea of Self and an identification with the objects of experience, there will be bondage. When we hold on and dress ourselves with the World, then Being becomes the World, the Being becomes the Self. When we realize our independence from the World, then we become centered in Being: we are whole, in peace, and immutable. Although there are many paths up the mountain of Freedom, the only summit is Not-self: There must be a detachment from the World as a means of transcendence to Being. This has been the discovery of all spiritual traditions: It is the Dark Night of the Soul, the No-mind, the Silence in the Desert, the Tao.

With the Freedom procured from the release of the Self, true Authenticity becomes possible. Authenticity has been historically understood as being "true to oneself" and typically in opposition to authority. The idea goes back to the Age of Enlightenment (The Age of Reason, from the 14th through the 17th century) when the disenchantment with the Catholic Church—as result of flagrant corruption of religious leaders—the onslaught of the Black Plague, and the allure of the new scientific revolution, inspired a reliance on reasoning and the importance of the individual. This emphasis on self-realization and self-expression has since then strongly influenced all facets of western society up to the present. Since then, to be authentic has meant to be your Self, as one who is moved by personality and passion rather than the values and opinions of others, or norms of society. We see, for example, a dramatic transformation of the decorative symphonies of Joseph Hayden into the tumultuous emotional autobiographical symphonies of Beethoven; in painting, from the representational melodramatic art of the Baroque era, to the extremely passionate and tragic paintings of Vincent Van Gogh.

Yet, as we have already learned, there is no real or true Self, but only a self-construct, forged out of ideas and emotions, with no substance. The Self, we discovered, is volatile, ever-changing, and irreducible to an essence. Therefore, any attitude stemming from the Self, coming across as any kind of character or personality, will be a convention, a contrivance, an unreality, and a most significantly, a condition which eclipses our true freedom. In other words, we don't become authentic by acting authentic.

Authentic happiness follows naturally out of the transcendence of the Self. Then our contentment is not as a result of something we desire, or something we believe in, or someone we must become, but derived from the spontaneity of unencumbered Being. This pre-reflective authenticity has transparency, a simplicity, and directness which is only colored by an individual learned style of communicating. Such a person is easy going, accepting, trusting, approachable, non-judgmental, and spontaneous; having no self-identity to protect, all affronts or flatteries go right through—have no place to land. She/he comports with awareness, with heedfulness, wisely choosing, not reacting.

We are led to believe by our hype-driven media culture that you must have a striking personality to be "somebody." Television actors, movie stars, athletes, musicians, and many other media celebrities all try to entice our attention with their charisma. It is what keeps them popular and making a profit—which is great for them—but it exaggerates the importance of "personality", of being someone special, of being a special Self. In reality, media stars are acting, playing at being spectacular, glamorous, fascinating; it is all a show, as their personal lives often reveal. One day somebody is a waiter, the next day after being "discovered" he/she is a superstar, and everyone wants a piece of their clothing and psyche. There is much happiness and peace of mind in being nobody, in just Being. Excitement, fame, and glamor do not last; these are treacherous fantasies that at any time can drop you from great heights into great anguish.

Being is not being anything; it is like a center around which everything turns; it does not change, run out, or fade away. It is difficult to imagine not being anything if you are continuously on the go, constantly entertaining yourself, always reaching for the next thrilling experience. Yet, there is a fullness, a subtle joy, contentment, a peacefulness, in just being-there, that does not feel like an emptiness or nothing.

We are told that before he was enlightened, Gautama the Buddha became an ascetic and disciplined himself severely, physically and mentally, coming close to dying. He was trying, like many of the religious adventurers of his time, to transcend the body towards a greater spirituality by torturing the flesh. Then one day, exhausted and emaciated from his efforts, he remembered the happiness he had experienced as a child while playing on the banks of the Ganges river, and this inspired him to a new beginning. What he remembered was the purity of the unencumbered mind of the young child: of a mind centered on its own Being. This most of us experience in our early years, but then it gradually fades away as formal education and the affairs of the world turn us into Selfs. The mind centered in Being, like the mind of a young child, is full of its own meaning-ness; it is free of the world and consummate in the pure joy of existing.

Being out of Time

We have all heard that we "should not live in the past," that we "cannot change the past," that we need to "let go of the past." Yet, despite all this useful worldly wisdom, most of us live as if slaves to the past.

But what is the past?

I know I woke up yesterday and brushed my teeth, had breakfast and went to work, then it was the evening, had dinner and went to bed, at the end of another day. Tomorrow I will most likely do most of the same things; and at present, I am writing this book. With the help of the sun, our watches, and cell phones, we are meticulously conscious of time, and as a result, we perceive our life as a process, with a beginning and an end. We know about time because we see all around us things that are moving and changing.

But now, let us imagine you are in a very dark room, sitting on a chair, with no sound, and no change in temperature. In this situation, what is it that you know? Having no discernment of day or night, you would lose track of the days and of the past, as everything would be just a dark present. You may notice your breathing, but it is a cycle (as in the movies, we will ignore the complications of eating and using the bathroom).a As you sit in the darkness, the only things that change are your thoughts, as they appear and disappear from consciousness in a sequence. Yet, since thoughts manifest at irregular intervals, they do not provide frame of reference for determining time. Furthermore, since to be able to recognize a series, to be conscious of it, one must occupy a point of view outside of it, the consciousness noting these changing mental objects must be in a timeless state. The One watching the thoughts does not move, cannot be measured: it is as if in the center of everything, as ever-present.

From the perspective of the dark room, it is easier to tell that time is a concept, it is a measurement. Time is the measurement in units of the change of something. It is a consciousness which does the measurement, that defines what time is, that gives time its existence. The reason we can determine time is precisely because we sit outside of the world; otherwise, we would not be able to see change—like being in the jumbo jet.

But now it gets even stranger! Because not only does consciousness create time, it also creates the universe. As we discussed earlier, each individual is a unique universe because each mind is a singular point of view observing the effect the material universe has on its own consciousness. Our consciousness brings things into being much like a floodlight revealing objects from an absolute darkness. Unlike the floodlight, however, nothing can be said to exist if the mind is not aware of it—it is as if the floodlight were not only drawing things out of darkness, but also into existence. For example, when you listen to music, the tones are understandable as melody and rhythm because consciousness gives the musical sounds structure and meaning as such: music exists only in the mind. In the same manner as consciousness causes sound to exist as music, so it also brings mathematics, physics, material things, the universe itself, into existence. It is not even that a computer, or mathematics, or the universe, are incomprehensible without a human mind, it is that they don't even exist. If you attempt at thinking of what there would be outside of conscious perception of the world, then you are already creating a conscious object of perception in your thinking about it. If you conceive that the universe could exist without anyone looking at it, it is because in your conception of this existing universe you are already positing yourself, or an imagined someone, as looking at it; or otherwise, you would need to concede that there is a creator who knows the universe to exist without humans or other conscious beings being aware of it.

The awareness of something, whether it is music, mathematics, or the universe of material things, always implies a knowing consciousness. Mathematics and physics are logical terms we use to describe our conscious experience of the universe. Although the physical universe reveals structure and laws, our mathematical and scientific understanding of it reflects how we are aware of it and are able to think about it, rather than what is really there. This is the reason why when you conform the universe to physics and mathematics, you get all kinds of fantastic theories which don't have much connection with reality—like Schrodinger's Cat.

Schrodinger's Cat is the name of a thought experiment designed by the physicist Erwin Schrodinger to illustrate the quantum nature of atomic particle. A cat is imagined in a box with a Geiger counter, a radioactive substance, a hammer, and a flask with poison. When the radioactive substance randomly releases a particle, the hammer falls, breaking the poison flask and killing the cat. Due to the unpredictable decay of the radioactive material, the cat exists both dead and alive (as a probability) until the box is examined; just like an atomic particle exists (mathematically) everywhere in a probability wave until measured. But now suppose that a robotic computer was to open the box and make a video of the cat. Could it be said the cat was alive or dead if no human—or another self-conscious being—ever observed the video? This further thought experiment particularly demonstrates what it means to be conscious of existence. Meaning that the cat does not actually exist, either dead or alive, until a human looks in the box. In our experience of existing, the universe *as we know it* comes into being.

Specifically, the past are thoughts we remember. Our history books are all the thoughts people have remembered. When I think of my past, I am only bringing up thoughts. What I did yesterday are thoughts that I am having in the present moment. When we think of an argument we had with our parents as a teenager, we are bringing up memory thoughts, with attached emotions. Even though it may seem like a matter of course that the past are thoughts, most of us experience our memories as if we are reliving the past: holding it, re-digesting it, regurgitating it. It is as if the past were to come alive again in the mind, like a TV re-run. What makes the thoughts come back, and seem alive, are the emotions still attached to unresolved situations. As long as we continue to embrace these thoughts as our past, as a past Self, they will continue to haunt us and overpower us—and grow our store of salt.

Modern wisdom encourages us to live in the present moment, forget the past, never mind the future, hold on to the now! But what is the present moment? As we have already seen, the past are thoughts of what happened, and the future are thoughts of what we imagine to be. The fact is that we cannot be anywhere else but in the present; all we do is change our focus from one thing to another. We focus on some idea, then focus on washing the dishes, then on a phone call we made, then an emotion, then on what we did yesterday, all occurring in the present moment. What it really means "to be mindful of the present moment" is to be aware of our objective point of view with regards to the World: as if at a distance, as a stepping back, from the objects of our consciousness. More accurately, there is no present moment, only a centered, time-less, personal awareness of the changing universe. Our actual experience of life, of existence, is not like a process, with a beginning and an end—that is only how we think of it—but more as the still center around which the World changes.

As long as we continue grasp at our thoughts as a past, or as a future, as who we are, as the Self, there will be no rest, no relief from the stress of life; the mind will be dragged along by the changing things of the World: a slave to time.

Being and *That*

We did not create ourselves. Although we are a Freedom, a Meaningfulness, a Being, these, as expressed by the philosopher Karl Jaspers (b.1883, d.1969), have been "given to us." There is *That* which is the foundation of our Being, which is beyond the World, beyond our ability to speak or even think about it. To that foundation we have given many names throughout time; but what is a name but of something of the world, and how do we think but with the things of the world, and what is it that we can know but only the world.

We cannot talk about *That* which is beyond the World without bringing *That* into the world. We can use the word God as a sign indicating "that which is the origin of all that exists." But to endow this God with any attributes is to make *That* in our image: for *That* is beyond male or female, finite or infinite, time and space, beginning and end, and all other earthly ways of thinking about it. For this same reason, there can never be proof of the existence or non-existence of God, because all that we can ever think about is what exists within our personal universe. Even the word *Creator* is corrupt with human understanding. "God" as a designation, therefore, must be made into an empty word, a hallowed word, meaning nothing to anyone who utters it. Our attitude towards *That,* can only be one of Faith: A Faith founded on the certitude of our Being.

We can ascertain the existence of *That* because of the certainty our Being, and because of the certainty of our contingency (that we know we did not create ourselves); and this knowledge is already a transcendence of physical existence. Here, it is in our Nothingness where we come closest to God:

This ultimate can be attained only in the transcending of all thought. It cannot itself be transcended. Before it lies contentment with one's lot and the extinction of all desires. Here is a haven and yet no fixed home. Here is a repose that can sustain us amid the inevitable unrest of our wanderings in the world. Here thought must dissolve into radiance. Where there is no further question, there is also no answer. In the philosophical transcending of question and answer we arrive at the limit, at the stillness of being (Jaspers 1951).

It is in our Nothingness, in the emptiness of Not-self, untouched by the ignorance and temptations of the World, where the essence of Being-as-*That* can flourish. It is from the unfathomable depth of Being-as-*That* where the inspirations of beauty, of true happiness, civil freedom, dignity, justice, sympathy, forgiveness, love, hope, our indubitable sense of existence, and our intuitions of God spring forth transcending our animal-ness and striking root upon the intellect.

God is not waiting for us in the silence of the mind. There is nothing in the silence of the mind but only silence. Being-as-*That* is being there, present, at once in the world and beyond it in Being:

Apart from the pulling and hauling stands what I am,
Stands amused, complacent, compassionating, idle, unitary,
Looks down, is erect, or bends an arm on an impalpable certain rest,
Looking with side-curved head curious what will come next,

Both in and out of the game and watching and wondering at it.
(Whitman 2004)

Our Freedom is the seal of our creator. Nothing but a foundation in absolute Freedom can justify the profound extent of human struggle, suffering, and hope. Nothing but a foundation in absolute Freedom can justify a non-intervention and be a testament to a perfection of creation. It is within an exigency of absolute Freedom that evil, as a manifestation of ultimate ignorance, can be comprehended and vindicated. It is the within the Freedom of Nothingness where authentic free will can exist.

We have been given all we need for our consummation. We have the world to satisfy our physical necessities, the awareness of our existence, and morality as our compass. Nothing else is needed; what more is there to ask for?

The transcendence of the World is wrought to completion through the transcendence of suffering. It is not through denial nor by stoic acceptance but by a transmutation of suffering as Not-self, that we arrive at essential Meaning.

Our Meaning is commensurate with our Being. Meaning is conspicuous in our good works done well, in the perfection of the arts and sciences, in great acts of athleticism; it conforms to truthfulness, honesty, justness, and an integrity of character. Meaning resonates in the heart with the selfless struggle: in the overcoming, the rising above, and in the going beyond the Self in the care of others. Yet, the greatest Meaning resonates with God, as *That,* in the emancipation of Being.

Letting Go

Letting go of something that bothers us or stresses us would seem like an easy thing to do—especially of something that is not ours to begin with; but, like most things in life and love, few things are ever as simple as they seem. So, it should not come as much surprise that the only way to really let go is through acceptance.

We have learned that our mental suffering is precipitated by sustaining in mind something which we simultaneously want and do not want, thus creating mental conflicts and strain. The reason that we find it so difficult to let go of these conflicting desires is that they constitute the matter of the Self which we strive to protect at almost any cost. Although we need the Self in order to interact in the world, if we take it too seriously, if we identify with it as to who we are, then it becomes a heavy albatross.

The Self is not something, not an entity, not a person; rather, an amalgam of thoughts and emotions which we have accumulated over our lifetime through our interaction with the world, which we then formulate into a general concept of who we are. This Self is not only comprised of conscious thoughts but also of subconscious thoughts and emotions, which erupt into full awareness with confrontations. What keeps the Self alive is the energy of emotions: The Self feeds on emotions. The Scottish philosopher, David Hume (b.1711, d.1776), observed that the vast majority of us are ruled by our emotions. We make emotional choices and then rationalize them to our convenience. Emotions are thoughts charged with mental energy, that become stronger and more tenacious with the more attention we give them. We employ these psychic-energy laced thoughts to protect our Self against the ever-present onslaught of the world, to reaffirm and assert its existence. So, for example, if someone accuses you making a mistake at the office, then anger emotions arise to protect the Self from losing self-esteem or becoming vulnerable to further aggression. If you hold strong beliefs or opinions, political or religious for example, then these will need to be defended against the opinions and judgement of others which threaten to undermine your integrity. If you have been a victim of neglect or abuse, then your injured ego will be vulnerable to the intimate approach of others, perhaps triggering suppressed memories from childhood or of a traumatic incident, which will then incite a slew of self-defending emotional tactics. Our fears, prejudices, and emotions keep us holding on to our Self for dear life.

Once you have developed strong mindfulness while in daily activity, then it becomes possible to identify the various manifestations of the egos as you move into different environments. Most frequently egos emanate with some emotion or some attitude, an acting out—especially the sexual ego which appears as if possessed. The experience of the Self, however, is more ambiguous, not characterized by outright reactions or emotions like the egos, but encountered more as a basic disposition or temperament, an underlying sense of Me. You may feel as a friendly, happy, positive Self, for example, or see yourself as an honorable and just person, or identify your-Self with a "young at heart" attitude. Some may stubbornly hold on to a destructive Self—such as in depression, sadism, chronic anger, or anorexia—because it feels like home.

If you feel that you can't live without your Self, then you should reconsider which Self it is you want to live with, because we reincarnate through many Selves since childhood. We call these phases, developmental stages, or facets of life. The reality is that the cute innocent 5-year-old is not the same person that becomes the rebellious teenager, nor the later responsible parent. They are different persons, with different minds and different bodies. Everything which determines our Self-identification changes as we grow older: the body, emotions, and mentality. The one thing that remains immutable throughout our lifetime is the Being, the point of view at the center of all these incarnations.

Even though the conflicts generated by our identification with the Self, and its projected egos, are a source of suffering and unhappiness, we cannot let go of the Self as an entity: because it is not an entity. Therefore, to dismantle our dependence on the Self, we must focus on its constituent parts: our identification with the physical body, sensations, thoughts, and emotions. We do this is by first realizing their objective existence and then deactivating them through acceptance.

To recognize and develop an objective perspective on the constituents of the Self, to realize a psychological distance from these, the practice of mindfulness and concentration meditation have proven the most efficacious. With concentration meditation we learn to quiet the mind sufficiently to recognize its independence from the objects it is conscious of: the body, thoughts, emotions, and sensations. This allows for the peacefulness and alertness necessary for the mind to withdraw from the World, to achieve at a detached point of view on the Self. Mindfulness of everyday activities then attains this objective distance while active in the world. Once objectiveness (detachment) becomes established, then we can relax into a pre-reflective point of view and refrain from getting absorbed into the World as Self, or at least avoid lingering there. The details on how we do this we will examine in the chapter on meditation.

Let's say you were insulted by someone, maybe a coworker earlier in the day; the thought of it still makes you angry, makes you want to fight back against the aggression, against the abuse. In your mind, you persistently replay the thought-memory of the insult associated with the emotion of anger. The memory is a thought that you are directing the anger at, and it can be mindfully seen as just that thought; it will dissipate with time and with the attention to other thoughts. The anger can be examined separately as well, as a pressing energy, which increases with every remembrance of the insult and leaches on to anything or anyone that crosses your path. When isolated from the thought of the insult, when observed mindfully as only energy, then the power of the emotion begins to dissipate. Since the actual situation has passed, the anger is being directed, not at the person (since no longer present), but at the thought of the incident itself: it is the thought which is the real threat to the ego now. The ego is also experienced as a thought of yourself being insulted—in your mind, you can see yourself arguing with that other person, as if from behind or above. If you suddenly think of something else, for example, the showtimes for a movie you want to see, then the anger is latent for that period of time, until the thought returns.

Unfortunately, what occurs in real life is not as simple as this illustration. An insult may trigger subtle memories associated with many past experiences, even going back to childhood, unleashing a variety of emotions, as a result of the complex nature of the Self. Nevertheless, all will be tied to the thought of the insult and its prominent emotion, which will be present to the mind as an objective entity. With practice, the influence of thoughts and emotions on the mind weaken as the attentive concentration and autonomy of the mind increases.

The trick to letting go of the Self entails, not in analyzing the thoughts or memories or emotions as to their source or cause, as this can be a Gordian Knot, but in seeing that these are objects of consciousness, are Not-self, thus creating that distance which will mitigate their power. This means that we don't have to understand how or why we come to have these thoughts and emotions which bother and stress us, but just realize our independence from them.

The objects of our awareness (sensations, emotions, ideas, the physical world, and the body) always change because these are conditioned things. Conditioned things depend on multiple factors, or causes, for their existence, and therefore change with the changing causes. Conditioned things are what we manipulate through our interactions with the world, in our grasping and rejecting of the world. For example, let's say I ate a large cheese pizza all by myself, and as a result, I now have a huge stomachache. The stomachache has been conditioned by my gluttonous tendency, the physical nature of my abdomen, the ingredients of the pizza, with all their precursors (the milk, the cow, the wheat, etc.), and my lack of common sense. Therefore, even though I am the author of my stomachache, it will remain an object for me which will eventually change. It would be inaccurate to state that the stomach discomfort or my gluttony is not mine, as if it had been mysteriously thrust upon me, and I could just ignore it or deny its existence, because I brought about its existence, through my ignorance and lack of self-control; it is my contingency: it is my salt. Yet, the stomach irritation is an impermanent condition, which exists *as-not-of-my-essence*, as Not-self.

Now the stomachache is stressing me, I don't want it, and I am disappointed with myself for being so impulsive with food, and this is making me upset. These thoughts and emotions which arise are also conditioned by my eating the pizza and my ego response. The thoughts and emotions are of my doing as well and are also present as objects in my mind; they come and go depending on situations, on causes, and previous decisions which I have made. They will not go away by suppression, by thinking "I am not my thoughts," as this would be grasping the idea of "not being the thoughts."

When we have identified the World as Not-self, as separate from Being, then we are ready to let go of it. But how can we make an effort to get something out of the mind, when it is the attention, the focusing on it, which keeps things in mind. We have all experienced this problem when we hear a song which we don't particularly like, and it becomes increasingly annoying the more we try to block it out. We can try to suppress it by thinking of something else, whistling, throwing water in our face, but despite much mental effort, it keeps pestering us: because we keep bringing it to mind by trying to get rid of it. We discussed this simultaneous grasping and rejecting as that which stresses the mind and makes emotional conflicts linger. Such is the nature of consciousness, that to pay attention, to focus on something, is akin to grasping, and we can't let go of something by grabbing it.

Once a thought or emotion, or an annoying tune, takes over the mind, *acceptance* is required to draw off its energy—so it can go away. Acceptance is non-resistance: it is the natural disposition to the realization of the World-as-Not-self. Acceptance does not mean indifference, alienation or shyness; it is not letting someone or some situation walk all over you. Once we create an objective distance with mindfulness and realize that the World is not ours, that it is impermanent, and ultimately cannot fulfill us, then we start to lose our fascination and hunger for it, our obsessions with it, and our fear of it—we begin to loosen our grip. The world does not disappear, nor do we become insensitive or apathetic, when we let go of it; rather, we develop a deeper appreciation and sensitivity for everything because we are no longer afflicted or conflicted by it. With acceptance, we are centered in our Being, just observing what comes and goes in the mind, not taking anything personally, but seeing all things as objects separate from the mind. We still feel the World—the pain, the anger, the sadness, the love—but we don't make more of it than it is, we don't suffer it personally: it is what it is.

When dealing with lost love situations, acceptance becomes especially efficacious in dismantling conflicts. For example, when we have lost a loved one, we are both grasping the loving memory and rejecting the pain of loss. We can be mindful of the fact that what we are holding on to, and trying to get rid of, are the emotional thoughts—the loved one is no longer present. Then, we can accept the pain, as the consequence of the desire we have created, rather than fight against it. When we truly love, when we love someone for their own sake, it is easier to let go without suffering.

Understanding the World as Not-self bestows many powers: patience, forgiveness, equanimity, fortitude, sympathy, wisdom, and acceptance. Then we realize we do not have to fight the World, but just let it be. This is all that is necessary because by nature the World is impermanent, and the things of the World will dissipate on their own.

When we loosen our grip on the world, our desire and fear of it, then we attain a peace of mind which allows for the flowering of wisdom. For example, the reason work becomes burdensome is because we want to be doing something else, and as a result, grip that "not wanting to be here" attitude of mind: it is the nagging thought of not wanting to be there which causes the mental stress and tiredness associated with working—since for most occupations there is nothing physically or mentally injurious involved. However, if we consider the worthiness of taking responsibility for care of oneself and family, recognizing the serious consequences of unemployment, and realizing that everything we do, even sports and going on vacation, involve significant effort, then we can wisely accept the fact of "work" and avoid the mental exertion and stress of wishing we were somewhere else. Furthermore, if we consider the personal satisfaction of a job well done, the improvement in the lives of others, the wellbeing and happiness it may bring to someone, the sense of pride, and the financial benefits to self and loved ones, then work becomes a joyful and meaningful vocation. Acceptance is supported and facilitated by Wisdom. Wisdom is the clear comprehension of the World as it is.

Dealing with chronic pain is always stressful. However, if we fight against the pain by rejecting it, then we not only have to endure the physical pain but also suffer mental anguish—which may then lead to depression, anxiety, gastritis, high blood pressure, and other complications. We should try our best to mitigate physical pain with medication or therapy, but beyond this, we have to learn to "deal with it," accept it the best way we can—to this extent mindfulness and concentration meditation have proven efficacious.

Acceptance is non-resistance: it is an "it is what it is" attitude towards the nature of human existence, not mentally grasping at or pushing away, not making more of something than what it is. Psychologically we are then not dragged into stressful situations but contemplate situations as if from a distance, with composure and comprehension, acting to correct problems methodically, with self-restraint and benevolent intent. Then, the powerful emotions are at our disposal as instruments we can thoughtfully and responsibly use for the good of ourselves and others.

When we practice detachment without acceptance, we run the risk of sliding into nihilism or apathy. If we reject the World, then we become another Self, a Self that doesn't want the World. When we *realize* (not just understand) the World as Not-self, then we transcend it. We don't reject or fight against a World which is not of our nature; we rather accept it as a condition of our existence.

Life comes to meet us with its demands: we must eat, drink, find shelter, and get along with others, and do this with integrity and goodwill. As well, there will always be problems, stress, concerns: with family, with our children, our parents, about money, about meeting the demands of daily life; these cannot be done away with, for that is the nature of our existence. What we can accomplish is a non-identification, independence, a detachment from the World, so that we don't make more of it than what it is. With this understanding comes wisdom, a fearlessness, courage. When we let go of our demands on the world, then we find satisfaction; then you are just as pleased and satisfied when at a party, or watching fireworks, or at work, as you are sitting alone at home doing nothing. When we accept *what is* on its own terms, when we give up our resistance to the world, then we find a natural state of happiness in just Being.

The letting go of the world does not mean getting rid of everything you own, doing without your favorite things, living in austerity, or becoming an ascetic. Giving up something you desire is a sacrifice, not a letting-go—since there is still the desire there. Or to put it another way, if you don't like broccoli then there is no problem in giving it up. We hold on to the things we want, to the things that we think we need for our happiness. When we were children we were fascinated by cartoons, candies, sweet drinks, and dolls; as adults, we have outgrown these things. In the same manner, as we observe carefully, mindfully, the fleeting nature of all sense experience, the phantasmal aspect of emotions, the mutability of beliefs, perceptions, and values, and the natural deterioration of the body, then it is easy to see that these things are not worthy of our indulgence or devotion. Releasing our dependence on the Self is a maturing. It is a realization that we are more than the World: that our true nature transcends the physical world and even our thoughts and emotions. Then, we completely understand the foolishness of our worldly desires, and the stress and suffering which our grasping of these will cause. Once the fascination with the World subsides, once the identification with a Self seizes, then we realize that we have always been complete, that we are whole. Then what manifests is a transparency: a direct perception and response to the World with an authenticity of Being.

Right Mindfulness

Mindfulness has proven to be a very effective treatment method for a variety of psychological problems: for emotional disorders like depression and eating disorder, for stress reduction in the workplace, for pain management, and prison rehabilitation, to name a few. Generally described as "paying attention to the present moment in a non-judgmental way," and also as a "remembering to pay attention," it has sparked the imagination of psychologists, life coaches, and entrepreneurs, to such an excess, that some critics have come to call it Mac-Mindfulness.

So, let us first take a step back and re-examine what mindfulness is.

As we discussed in a previous chapter, the mind can only be in the present moment, that is, dwelling on the past or the future is just entertaining memories or imagination, and as a result, the instruction to be "mindful of the present moment" only lends confusion as to what we're supposed to be doing with our attention. What most practitioners end up doing when trying to be in "the present moment" is just being alert to physical sensations—the colors, the sounds, smells, tastes, etc.

Essentially, mindfulness is just *paying attention*: it is the ability of our mind to focus on something. It is what we do when we read a book, thread a needle, memorize a sentence, choose an avocado at the supermarket, etc. When we are not mindful, not focusing on anything, then we are lost in ever-proliferating thoughts without much attention to what we are doing or thinking about, emotionally reacting to whatever pops into our minds: we are lost in the World.

Where mindfulness becomes truly transcendent and therapeutic is when it is *mindfulness of the World as Not-self*, or mindfulness without identification. This is what the Buddha intended as Right Mindfulness. Here we hold the World out before us as an object, as at a distance (according to Sartre), to carefully study it and understand it clearly, rather than reacting to it with our ignorance and emotions. It is due to the nature of consciousness as being a Nothingness, because it exists as outside of the World, that we can do this. When we practice Right Mindfulness, we are no longer lost in the world of desires; we are no longer victims of our own ignorance. When we are mindful of thoughts as Not-self, as being objects of our consciousness, then we do not grab on to them, we don't become them, but are able to witness their true nature as impermanent phantasmal entities. When we are mindful of emotions as Not-self, they are not as threatening, not as dense and challenging; we can observe their energy as it dissipates like melting ice. In the same perspective, the body does not feel like Me, but as the extension of consciousness into the physical world, like a vehicle; then, my pains are not as personal, not as threatening, and no longer a source of mental suffering, my pleasures no longer enslaving.

For example, when we practice mindfulness of eating, we are attentive of the transient nature of food: of how it feels and tastes in the mouth, how it is chewed and swallowed, of how fleeting is the flavor. We eat with clear the comprehension, with the wisdom, that food is primarily for our nutrition. The pleasant taste we enjoy for what it is, a brief sensation, without deluding ourselves that it can be a source of fulfillment or happiness. It is in this manner that we arrive at moderation: choosing foods which are sufficiently palatable and beneficial to our health.

There is no point in trying to be overly mindful of the food itself—as if it were the last grape you will ever eat. It is sufficient to pay attention to the process of eating and that the food and the taste are objects of your awareness, are a short-lasting experience, and not conducive to happiness—just a momentary pleasure.

In practicing mindfulness of the body, we pay attention to our physical health, our appropriateness of dress, and the effect our body has on others. As discussed, it is predominantly by means of the body that we develop as individual conscious being, and thus it is important to take good care of it by eating healthy, exercising, and avoiding the ingestion of toxins. The mind and the body are closely linked, such that what affects one will impinge on the other: a healthy body will bolster a healthy, peaceful mind. The body is also our immediate means of expression. What we intend with the mind we exteriorize with the body. Clothing serves not only for the protection against the elements, but also to guard our sexuality and express our sense of modesty. We need to have a clear understanding of what we communicate to others with our clothing and mannerism, being aware of the consequences our decisions and actions will have on others and ourselves.

When practicing Right Mindfulness of the mind, we recognize the objective existence of our thoughts, perceptions, and emotions, and note their arising and dissolution. When we become adept at being mindful of the objects of the mind, it becomes painfully obvious how much time and energy we waist with unnecessary thinking, and how peaceful, quiet, and focused, the mind naturally is. We learn to control our emotions rather than inadvertently feed them. We are able to observe the emergence of desire, the energy with which the mind jumps to grab at things, and the power of its repulsion. With practice and time, the impulse to react to the world abates, and we develop a serene appreciation for beauty and composure in the enjoyment of the pleasures of the world. We can enjoy the beauty of objects, music, paintings, or people without the compulsion to possess them. We can experience unpleasant things and people without rejection or disgust.

To develop Right Mindfulness, you can practice breathing meditation as taught by the Buddha in the "Anapanasati Sutta." First, while sitting with the eyes closed, we focus on the process of breathing to calm the mind and establish an objective perspective on the World; then we observe the body, the feelings, emotions, and thoughts, with the ultimate goal of apprehending these as Notself. In the chapter on meditation, we will detail how to do this effectively.

Once you are able to observe your thoughts and emotions objectively, you will become acutely aware of the effect these have on your state of mind. Throughout the day you will experience how negative thoughts weigh down the mind, stress you, and how positive thoughts liven up your mood, make you feel lighter. While stronger thoughts will trigger emotional reactions, less potent negative thoughts, if persisting, will gradually affect your attitude and energy. At times you will notice how light and effortless your mind feels when you are not attending to any thoughts at all. With mindfulness of the mind, you can learn to restrain negative thoughts from prolonging and bolster positive thoughts and attitudes to improve your mood and physical energy. You will be acutely aware of the powerful effect thoughts have on yourself and others.

We can also practice walking meditation to develop mindfulness with activity. To do this we focus on the simple act of lifting and placing of the feet slowly over a short distance; as soon as you notice a thought intruding, you ignore it and focus back on the walking. This is usually practiced for about 10 mins between sitting meditations, or as long as you want.

Right Mindfulness opens the way for a realistic apprehension of our human condition. It does away with magical thinking based on naive perceptions of World-as-Self, which clouds our understanding and clutter our minds and conditions unwholesome reactions to the world and others. By paying correct attention to our perceptions and prejudices, we can start cleaning up the mess in our minds and realize a simple and peaceful way of living.

Right Parenting

Raising a child can be our most significant accomplishment and greatest reward, or our greatest failure and worse regret.

Although we were all children once, as adults we can hardly remember what it was like: the intensity with which the world revealed itself to us, the great joy in the simplest pleasures, the openness to life and others. Over time, as we grow older, our sensibilities dull. As our minds become increasingly cluttered with education and opinions, and as life becomes more rational and predictable, the world becomes more troublesome than beautiful, more threatening than wonderful. As we grow into adulthood, most of us conform to seeing the universe through the eyes of our parents, and as we become parents, we instinctively and indiscriminately adopt their prejudices, fears, and misperceptions, as what is most sensible in raising our own children.

Being a parent is a most wonderful thing.

Through the eyes of our child we again experience the wonder and joy of discovering the world. With each new experience, as when seeing a butterfly or a puppy or tasting ice cream, their curiosity and surprise resonates in us with nostalgia for when life was exciting and mysterious. The accepting smile, the guileless eyes, and the kind disposition of young children reflect a purity of spirit which is rare to chance upon at any other age. It is difficult to put into words the profound compassion a parent feels when witnessing the struggles and accomplishments of their child. The first words, the first steps, the first day at school, the winning score, the performance, the birthdays, the graduation, the wedding are things that mysteriously resonate in the heart of a parent. Their innocence and vulnerability inspire in us a most selfless love. With their playfulness and liveliness children gift us with a joy which is truly incomparable.

Being a parent is about being real.

The happiness of being a new couple seems to bloom naturally into a desire to be a parent. Then the sight of babies, baby clothes, little shoes, baby bottles, strollers, inspire a tenderness and a longing to hear the sweet cooing sounds of our own offspring. Other parents encourage us to start a family, recounting the wonders of pregnancy, the happiness of the baby shower, the joys of buying baby furniture and of painting the baby room.

Long forgotten by these veteran procreators are the cold realities of parenthood: the discomforts and complications of pregnancy (nausea and vomiting alone affecting 75%), the worries and complications of labor, postpartum depression (affecting up to 15% of mothers), awakening for feedings during the night every 2-3 hours for many weeks, the loss of personal time and freedom, and the loss of intimacy as a couple. The birth of a child does not strengthen a relationship but rather threatens to dismantle it. The reality is that what motivates most couples to have a baby is fantasy.

How we grasp the world to fill our emptiness is to a great extent through fantasies: the entertaining of unrealistic and overly optimistic ideas regarding a wish. We adhere to unrealistic ideas about employment, professions, family, people, marriage, about life and death, and about raising children. Marriage and parenthood are strongly fantasy driven. The high rate of divorce is evidence to the misapprehension that marriage is more about compromise, forgiveness, and understanding, than endless romance, orgasms, and living happily ever after. No less a great fantasy is parenting, with few people carefully planning for the stresses, responsibilities, and personal sacrifices which come with raising a child well. Perhaps it is this ability to fantasize which keeps the world moving and populated, but it frequently leads to disenchantment and suffering.

After the crude reality of the pregnancy, the delivery, and the first several months of babyhood, comes the no less daunting task of raising the child.

Being a good parent is about being responsible.

The mind of a child is pure Nothingness. While our genetic inheritance determines the sensitivities of an individual, that is, the degree of receptiveness and reaction to the internal and external environments, what we apprehend in the consciousness a young infant is a pure being-there. The young infant is all pre-reflective consciousness: there is awareness but no thinking, and therefore there is no Self. It is our great moral imperative *to do our best* to endow our child with a wholesome Self. To the degree we succeed and fail at this will be reflected in our own Self-respect: our integrity, peace of mind, and our happiness.

Although the greatest gift we can bestow our child—as you might guess by now—is not from the world, nevertheless, they do need the world in the right measure to develop a healthy mind. To this extent a good parent needs to provide for a child's physical needs, with the correct amount and quality of food (i.e., a balanced diet) and the proper amount exercise. Most important, child needs to feel protected, in a safe environment at home and at school. These obligations can be met by parent(s) at almost any economic level.

Because human consciousness is devoid natural inhibitions, since it is a total freedom, it is crucial that we provide a child with the right measure of discipline to foster self-control. By establishing

110

consistent rules and boundaries, and by applying suitable doses of gratification and punishment, we help the child develop and internalize restraints to his/her behavior, which is indispensable for a balanced, healthy sense of Self. That is, by saying "no" to a child, the child learns to say a "no" to him/her-self: internalizes inhibition. A child that grows without limits, without respect for rules nor personal boundaries, does not know who he or she is: The Self becomes an ambiguous and distorted entity, causing undue suffering to the child and others. To this extent, the great negligence of our times is not allotting for enough intimate attention and discipline for our children: too much T.V., too much electronic media, and too little personal interaction.

It is by way of personal interaction with a parent that an infant can identify a separate existence from the world, to determine a being-there, to engender a point of view on the World. Personal interaction between child and parents is then critical in the first two years of life for the child to develop a healthy, congruent, assertive Self. Prompt attention to the cries of the young infant reinforces self-existence and mitigates stress. In bestowing Self-awareness, eye contact is essential: the presence of the eyes, the Look, communicate a self-objectiveness to the infant, a being something—being a Me. But, no less important is talking. Personal words have a directness, a force of identification and reassurance, which is essential for successful bonding with the child and promoting self-esteem. The touching the body communicates affection, intimacy, and protection. The infant left to cry, not touched, not spoken to, not Looked with, develops an unstable, confused, frustrated Self; a Self always hungry for reassurance, for recognition, and intimacy.

By the time we become parents most of us have forgotten what it was like to be a child, how it felt to discover the world, and how we idolized our parents as our own personal heroes—as superhuman beings. As we grow older, the flaws of those who care for us became increasingly apparent: the lax integrity, the imperfect honesty, the weakness of character, and for some, the outright cruelty. With time, as we become the heirs of their salt, the disenchantment and disappointments with our parents become the justification for our own shortcomings.

We are the prime and the most important teacher of our children. Children learn by observing their parents; they walk, talk, and gesture like their parents; they absorb our values even if they seem to rebel against them; they integrate our way of thinking and our emotional sensitivity. They are the heirs of our salt and water.

With our children, we have the opportunity to do better, to change the future, to dilute the salt. With careful mindfulness of our thoughts, our emotions, our actions, and reactions, we gain a healing perspective; and in healing our own minds, we heal the ones who love us, who look up to us, and who depend on us for their wellbeing. We can be mindful of our motivations and fears; of the memories and emotions which are triggered by situations or by their misbehavior; of our own reactions and the appropriateness of our punishments. We should be keenly aware of the importance we give them as individuals, the respect we render them, while maintaining the integrity and respect of the parent-child relationship: love them and respect them but let them know who is boss. Most of all, we must bestow them intimate personal attention. We need to model for them integrity, self-respect, respect of others, honesty, and sincerity. We must assure them of being cared for and loved. We can be authentic heroes for them!

With human beings, however, 2+2 will almost invariably not equal 4. What ultimately becomes of an individual is individual, and therefore, beyond anyone else's resolve or control; as each of us has a personal road to travel and personal choices to make. We can only do our best to help our children become an upright, happy persons. But to do our best to help them, we must be Real with ourselves first. We must make a heroic commitment to do our best by them. We will only be held morally accountable for the negligence of doing the right thing. It is in this that our children gift us with the opportunity to accomplish the ultimate act of true love and personal fulfillment: to give of ourselves selflessly for the sake of others.

III

Being

Authentic Happiness

While you will attain much happiness and peace of mind from fostering positive attitudes and not indulging negative intentions, because these hinge on a changeable World and your Self, there will inevitably be backsliding and disappointment. We discovered that the primordial condition of our unhappiness and suffering is our Nothingness. This fear of being nothing, of our existential emptiness, is what coerces us to grasp the World as Self in an attempt to become some-thing. Therefore, this identification with a Self, even a positive one, will always be a burden, an obstacle, an unreality—in Bad Faith.

When we realize that the Self is the thoughts and emotions which we are accustomed to grasping, and that we are an absolute subjectivity observing the World as from a distance, then we are on the way to realizing unconditioned Freedom and Authentic Happiness. From this perspective, we are empowered to release our negative thoughts and emotions, and to nurture benevolent, wholesome intentions. Then, with each virtuous deed and with each act of love and kindness, we mindfully add more and more water to our salt.

When we are free from having to be anything, free from the influence of any Self, then we can dwell in the tranquility of the unencumbered mind. Then we become skilled in feeling and recognizing the heaviness, the strain, of negative thoughts and emotions, and we are able to release them quickly and effortlessly. We can enjoy the lightness, the uplifting-ness, of wholesome thoughts, without the need to indulge them.

By now you may have figured out that there is nothing which we are destined to accomplish in the world, no grand master plan for which we are personally responsible for. No matter how talented you are, how many things you've accomplished, and how much you have learned, the truth is that it will all come to an end, with the end of your World. No matter how long humankind survives, this solar system will end, this galaxy will end, and this universe will end. Our happiness and meaningfulness, therefore, cannot hinge anything of the World.

Yet we are in the world for a purpose. There are no "accidents" in the universe for the simple reason that everything is dependent on, is contingent on, previous conditions regressing back to the beginning of time. Everything in the universe has a previous cause, and even though we may not comprehend a first cause, we know that we are moving, and we KNOW that we are here. And this knowing is already a transcendence of our earthly existence.

We are as if thrown into a world which is foreign to our nature, like onto an ocean without knowing how to swim, and must take up our responsibility for doing our best to survive and do well by it. We must take responsibility for the care of our body and our family, and for others with whom we share this life; take care of the animals and the natural environment; and, it is in this caring that we find meaning and achieve personal growth in the world.

Authentic happiness is not about feeling joyful all the time nor having a predisposition to wellbeing; it is not about having a hypersensitive state of awareness nor frequent pleasurable experiences;

you can't get to it with fame, fortune, power, or knowledge; all these are impermanent, conditioned states and therefore incompatible with long-lasting, meaningful happiness. In fact, true happiness is not about any special thing or experience. Although most people believe that they will be happy if some condition or problem in their life is resolved—like having more money to pay off bills, having more free time, a successful career, the return of a loved one, or overcoming a severe illness—this will only bring temporary satisfaction, a short-lived relief. Anything which we desire of the World, any object, feeling, emotion, idea, an idea or desire for happiness, will be something outside our control, not lasting, and an eventual source of unhappiness. You will not be authentically happy by becoming something.

Our search for happiness is in effect a quest for our true self. When the mind is empty of Self, when there is no self-reference to our intentions, when there is no Self to measure things for or against, when there is nothing to protect, then we are thoroughly liberated into Being. Authentic Happiness issues from that state of non-attachment to the World, which is an absolute Freedom, a centeredness in Being. It is this that achieves true peace of mind. This Being, this ultimate reality, is WHO WE TRULY ARE; it is not something we know; it is something we live.

We are different from the rest of the universe because we know that we exist. This certitude of existence is our experience of Being. This assuredness of existing, this knowing, is not some chemical reaction, some alchemic effect of neural matter, and not an illusion. It is a singularity, a meaningfulness, and it is what gives everything else in the world its meaning. Being is like a luminescence which brings reality to everything it shines upon, bestowing existence onto everything. It is a witnessing of the universe.

It is not in the world where we find our purpose; it is our Being which fills the world with purpose!

Releasing our identification with the Self is not easy. It takes practice, perseverance, courage, and faith, to relax into Nothingness: into just Being. It is like learning to float on the ocean: you don't do, you let go, you relax into it. Releasing the Self is like dropping a heavy stone that you have been carrying all your life, thinking it is your child. At first, when you stop holding on to thoughts and memories, the body, the emotions, you feel a growing restlessness: this is the dawning of the Nothingness. You feel a compulsion to do something, that you are wasting your time, feel as if disoriented, with a kind of existential vertigo. But if you stay with it, then the mind releases, it stops trying to go somewhere, and you suddenly experience a wonderful peacefulness: like you will never need anything ever again.

The Nothingness and temporariness of human life on Earth does not mean that it would be best to do nothing, or that human life is meaningless: that would be nihilism. Quite the contrary, once we realize the unconditioned meaningfulness of Being, everything that exists for us becomes resplendent with that same meaning. All our activities take on a higher value because they are inspired by authentic creativity, rather than by a desire for fame and fortune. We are motivated to do our best as parents, spouses, workers, artists, scientist, without grasping these as foundations of meaning, as our reason for existing, but from a simple inspiration of living.

The happiness of Being is subtle. When you become unfettered from the World, liberated from the Self, there are no fireworks, no mystical or esoteric experiences, no acquisition of supernatural powers: there is just the centeredness, the peacefulness, the meaningfulness. If you have been very attached to the world, or living mostly in your thoughts, or very dependent on others, then the sudden dissolution of the Self can be a profound experience: the total freedom, the opening up, the release of the mind, can feel like a mystical experience—a consuming joyfulness. But this joyfulness is not home, and it will not last; it is a way home to the happiness, equanimity, and peacefulness of Being.

Authentic Happiness is the peace of mind that issues from un-encumbered Being. Then life becomes simple. We are no longer running around indulging in excitement or adventure and then suffering the withdrawals. Instead, we find that it doesn't take much to be happy. A simple home cooked meal, taking a walk, even doing the dishes, take on a new meaning. We comprehend and appreciate material wealth, entertainment, travel, or sex, for what it can genuinely afford: temporary pleasures not worth stressing over, or sacrificing for, or planning your life on. We acquire a simple, straightforward, nonjudgmental attitude towards people. We enjoy a genuine conversation, rather than aiming to persuade, entertain, argue, compete with, or impress others. Life becomes simple, uncomplicated, centered, and balanced; one is satisfied with the happiness of just Being.

Nothing Meditation

Meditation is always mindfulness meditation. We are using the ability of our awareness to focus attention, to observe the objects of the mind. Yet, while other forms of meditation use this ability of consciousness to promote relaxation or manipulate mental habits, our final destination will be the emancipation of Being—this occurring in the milieu of quiet sitting. We will direct our attention to investigate the World as object, to create a distance from the World, so that we can scrutinize it carefully and thoughtfully without getting involved in it. Our goal is to release the World (the physical world, the emotions, thoughts, and memories) as Not-self. When this occurs, then a recognition of Being naturally emerges.

Even though we all share the same facial and body features, and the same way of being conscious, we are at the same time different in our appearance, and in how we perceive and react to the world—like music, generating an infinite variety of melodies from the same twelve basic tones. Similarly, with meditation, we should expect to have different manifestations relative to our sensibilities and life experience.

Nothing Meditation

We will make use of the breathing meditation technique as described by the Buddha in the "Anapanasati Sutta" to distill the essential nature of our Being: what the Buddha formulated as Not-self. Although breathing meditation has been widely used to attain enlightenment, the original teaching from the sutta has been over time muddled with opinions and misunderstanding, making the practice unnecessarily cumbersome and mostly ineffective. It is not uncommon to find that despite many years of training with breathing meditation many practitioners grow frustrated and disillusioned at the lack of fruition or substantial benefits. The principal reason for this is due to a misunderstanding of the ultimate objective of the sutta. Following the same principle waiting on lines, where everyone gets in the longest line just because it is the longest, many aspirants follow well-worn paths misleading them to an attachment to meditation, to false expectations, or to achieve some fantasy of earthly bliss. As a result, many become disheartened, feeling that attainment of enlightenment is only for the very few who have a lot of free time, like the monks, or those blessed with supramundane talents.

The main obstacle in application of the principles of the sutta is in making too much out of it, rather than following the instructions of the Buddha quite literally as presented. Here, our concern will be with keeping it simple.

While it is not terribly important how you sit to meditate, as this will not affect the outcome of the meditation, you basically don't want to be either too comfortable or too uncomfortable. To accomplish this, it is usually sufficient to sit comfortably upright in a chair, without reclining; or better, if possible, to sit in the half-lotus, yoga position: sitting on a 5-10 inch wide cushion, with the lower legs folded-in one on top of the other on the floor, and the hands resting one on top of the other in the center. The back should be comfortably straight, without straining. The half-lotus position is the right balance between comfort and discomfort and provides a sort of "mood" for what is going to happen—like being in a ready position to run a race or waiting to hit a tennis ball. You should experiment until you find your somewhat comfortable position.

Once a semi-comfortable sitting position is achieved, then we should focus on the general awareness of the breathing. The best object for calming and focusing the mind is *the breathing*, not the breath. Following the breathing, we *know* when we are breathing in and *know* when breathing out. You don't need to control the breathing or give it too much importance, but just be aware of it, just know it—it is pretty straightforward to know that you are breathing. If you try to focus the breath on your nose, or abdomen, or diaphragm, then it becomes mindfulness of nose, abdomen, or diaphragm, instead of the breathing. We want to focus only on the experience of breathing, on its immediate reality, with the intent of calming the thoughts and emotions so we can apprehend them as Not-self. Although it is traditionally referred to as concentration meditation, with breathing meditation we strengthen both our ability to concentrate and our mindfulness.

Knowing the breathing should be easy and relaxing. *Here there is nothing else to do with your awareness than know the breathing and everything else which appears as the World, as an object that you are looking at, as Not-self.* If a thought appears—e.g. of plans, a song, memories of a conversation, or scenes from a movie—you simply know that a thought has emerged and recognize its object-ness; then it will fade away as the attention returns to the breathing. Some persons may experience colored clouds, or a white light, or other obscure mental objects; these are not an omen or signs of anything, just manifestations of a deepening concentration, just more objects that are Not-self—anything which you can observe is not you. As the great Theravada teacher, Ajahn Chah commented: breathing meditation should be like going on a peaceful vacation, with nothing to do or to think about, just letting go of all concerns.

Nothing Meditation

While you are focusing on the breathing, any physical sensations which attract your attention should be known as Not-self: as an object of awareness. For this, I suggest just noting what can be directly experienced as a sensation, instead of taking a relaxation inventory of the body. Unless you have a particular physical illness or injury, you would not be aware of much more than whatever stimulates the skin (an itch, coolness, warmth), the pressure of your weight on the buttocks, the position of the legs, and perhaps a slight discomfort from the sitting position. If you feel muscle tension, then you should relax it, noting its objective quality. If you make a relaxation inventory of the body, then you will most likely be focusing on mental images and not on the sensory experience of the body itself—that is, if you concentrate on the breath or some energy as flowing through your body, then you will be grasping at mental images, desires, and expectations, rather than experiencing the body as simply Not-self.

The purpose of mindfulness meditation on the body is basically to *know* the body as Not-self: to fully realize the perception of the body as an object, as distinct from your point of view, as not being your true essence. Whatever manifests, whether discomfort, an itch, a numbness, this is seen as Not-self, as just something you are observing, something with a transient existence. It is enough to experience the body simply as it is. Putting up with some discomfort as a test of your endurance is an attachment to ideas. As Gautama the Buddha painfully discovered, there is no purpose or benefit in torturing the body.

With the same understanding, we do not need to be overly concerned with the surrounding environment if it is moderately comfortable and not too distracting. If you try to find a perfectly quiet place to meditate, then you will most likely be frustrated in your effort—and if you find it, you might fall asleep. If there is the noise of construction, or a dog barking, or a door slamming, then this is just another object for the mind to observe (as sound) and not grasp, not make anything of it, but just know it; any emotional reactions to distractions would be only more objects to identify as Not-self. Whatever comes up in the world, we plainly and mindfully accept as Not-self—nothing else to do.

The more we practice seeing everything as Not-self, the more obvious it becomes that the World is other than the consciousness, we, that is looking at it; the objective distance becomes greater.

Some teachers emphasize what is called Jhana, or absorption, as the principal objective of breathing meditation, or even as a requisite for Enlightenment. Absorption occurs when the mind becomes so profoundly focused on the breathing that all other perceptions disappear, even of the breathing, eventually only remaining awareness of awareness. Some Jhana enthusiasts report remaining in this state of suspended animation for hours, some even days, barely breathing and with a minimal pulse. After coming out of Jhana, practitioners usually report feeling a serene joyfulness and a detachment from the world which may last for days. The only complication with this experience is that however wonderful it may be, it will not last forever; soon the world will return with its problems and demands to darken the illumination, leaving the practitioner yearning for another great trip. While the experience of Jhana, in moderate doses, is invaluable in fomenting a sense of emancipation from the World and in helping to identifying Being, if overemphasized, it will pose a risk of attachment and disenchantment; so that, if you have never attained Jhana then you will feel that you are not making progress and become disheartened; and if you have had a blissful experience, then you will be disappointed if it does not recur, or yearn for more when you are out of it. Furthermore, some practitioners may even confuse Jhana with enlightenment, causing undue confusion and disappointment.

The purpose of mindfulness of breathing, or concentration meditation, is to provide a steady uninteresting object for the mind to focus on and not get lost grasping and becoming anything which pops into the field of awareness. It is a rudder to steady the mind with, to get your awareness from deviating into thoughts. It is not a club to beat down your thoughts with; this would be suppression of the objects of the mind and will lead to stress and anxiety.

When you first start to practice, the mind will quickly get bored or habituated with the monotonous breathing and readily latch on to any thought, memory, or emotion and go with it. With patience, practice, and motivation, however, you will begin to recognize that your awareness of the thoughts does not change as the thoughts are changing: you begin to identify your point of view as the center, and everything else that you can be conscious of as what is changing around you.

Nonetheless, initially the breathing may feel heavy and forced, and you may experience itching, or throat discomfort, or other bodily sensation, but once the attention is unwavering, the breathing will slow down, becoming relaxed and enjoyable. As you begin to identify thoughts as objects and not get involved with them, your awareness becomes more adept at staying with the respiration, and the thoughts and other mind objects become less tempting and frequent. Your understanding, and wisdom, regarding the nature of human existence—the unreality of the Self, and the impermanent and unsatisfying nature of the World—will be instrumental in cultivating this disinterest. Eventually, as the thoughts stop appearing, the mind will relax and settle with the breathing into an awareness of an agreeable peacefulness. This intrinsic peacefulness then becomes the new focus of attention.

When all my thoughts stop, I am only aware of my breathing, but it feels as if disembodied, as I have lost contact with all the other senses: it feels as if it is my mind that it is now barely breathing. Then, I am relaxed and content witnessing the peacefulness of the mind. Here, I can decide to completely let go of the breathing and become wholly immersed in the experience of pure awareness, as Jhana, or remain within the perspective of Not-self. In the former, there is no perspective on anything, and I am totally absorbed into the pleasant awareness of pure existing, my consciousness is pure subjectivity; in the latter, I am aware of Being, as an awareness of existing as separate from my consciousness of the World. While both experiences are helpful, it is the experience of Being which I can bring back to the mundane world. This experience of Being is neither subtle nor obscure, but rather an awareness of the immense power of existing.

Once you have become adept at calming the mind and not grasping your thoughts during meditation, then I recommend practicing Nothingness Meditation. Nothingness Meditation entails doing nothing. It is just sitting anywhere for whatever time you have available and attending to nothing but your consciousness of existing—again, as a verb. Here, to nurture this discernment, you can start by asking yourself, "how do I know I exist," until you arrive at the that essential experience of existing. This practice is advantageous, for one thing, to avert the grasping of concentration meditation and mindfulness practice as an identity, as something special you do. And, since no special wardrobe or practice hall is needed, it does not impress as being something esoteric, or as only for special people.

With Nothing Meditation, you are not following your breath or doing anything special, but simply disregarding anything which comes to mind, any thought, or any urge to do something; all is seen as Not-self and let pass. This is auspicious to recognize that urge of the mind to keep occupied, to do something. It is like a mini mental vacation. I keep my eyes open, gently observing whatever is present, but without elaborating any thoughts about what I see. I don't suppress my thoughts or focus on my breath intentionally. Any thoughts that comes to mind I know it as a fabrication, an impermanent entity—as a ghost of the mind—and it doesn't last long. After a while, you develop an increased appreciation and sensitivity for the lightness and clarity of pure consciousness, in contrast to the heaviness of thoughts, the irritation of emotions, and the exhausting grasping of things. I am only aware of being aware. Being is enough.

Concentration meditation should not be practiced while doing anything that requires alertness to a situation, like driving, working, or taking care of children. For example, if you are driving then you should be practicing mindfulness of driving—grasping and being very attentive to what you are doing. Also, Mindfulness meditation is not being absorbed in any activity to the point that you forget yourself in what you are doing, that is just getting lost in the world as the Self—what we usually do. Mindfulness Meditation is being conscious of meticulously seeing the World as other, as Not-self.

The outcome of concentration meditation is a cleansing of the mind; it is purged of the World for a while. During concentration meditation, the mind is peaceful and content, full of itself, resting in Being. Once the World returns, everything is the same except for a change in our perspective. We are now mindful of the World as from the *outside*, from the point of view of Nothingness, looking at a World that is Not-self. This realization of Being as apart from the World is Enlightenment: It is the beginning of the process of healing.

While you will attain significant mental health and, as a result, great peace of mind by being mindful of your thoughts and respecting the Red Rule, there will still be a degree of stress, confusion, and suffering if you identify with a Self. There is a greater reality, a greater peace and fulfilment, which is realized with the permanent release of the Self: this is the cessation of all ill will, all ignorance, and all suffering: this is the Unbinding.

Enlightenment and Unbinding

Enlightenment follows from not being the World, or as Sartre considered, from the nihilation of the World from consciousness. Consequently, it is easier to discuss what Enlightenment is not.

For many traditions, Enlightenment is the fruition of a process of transformation. It is generally described as an awakening. In this sense, it indicates a coming out of darkness, as in opening the eyes to a new day, a clear seeing; and in this sense, it is misleading. There is nothing spectacular that happens with enlightenment, everything will be the same, just the point of view changes, from the Self to the Not-self. By calling this transcendence of the Self an Enlightenment or Awakening, something that is not so difficult to achieve is misrepresented as abstruse, mystical, and esoteric.

The enlightenment of Enlightenment has more to do with mentality than anything else. If you have developed a habit of thinking too much, of worrying, of holding on to your World to feel secure, then when you finally let go of it, it will feel as if you were born again. If you have been chronically depressed, or angry, or overly sentimental, then you live with strong emotional attachments, and releasing your grip on these will make you feel like you have come close to heaven, light and peaceful. If you are generally easygoing and relaxed, where nothing really rocks your boat, then releasing the World will feel more natural, as a profound peacefulness, but without bells and whistles.

Enlightenment is not the conclusion of the effort to liberate the mind, it is not the final frontier. Understanding this is critical because many practitioners experience profound mental clarity and peacefulness after releasing the World and believe that this enlightenment is Liberation (or Nirvana); then become frustrated, depressed, and disenchanted, when the problems and stresses of the world, like dark clouds, come creeping back into the mind.

Enlightenment can be best understood as the realization of not being the World: the sudden realization of a point of view outside of the World. It is the expulsion (nihilation) of the World from consciousness. Suddenly I apprehend that everything I see, everything I know, is not what I am, but are all objects of my awareness, and I am the emptiness of everything. We can call this an Enlightenment in pointing to this profound, all at once insight into the nature of human existence. We can call it Original mind because it is the essential nature of the unencumbered consciousness. It is emptiness because consciousness is not anything, and since the World is made out of consciousness, it is as well an emptiness: all is emptiness.

But even though I am the negation of the World as Not-self, a Nothingness, I am not non-existence, for it is I, by means of my self-consciousness, who does the negating, the nihilation. This emptiness of the World which I am, I am as Being. This Being is the indubitable certitude of my existence, all at once unfathomably profound and terribly mundane. What makes Buddhism impenetrable for many, and makes many interpretations incomplete and unnecessarily esoteric, is the misunderstanding of the Not-self doctrine as being the consummation of the path: what becomes, rather, an attachment to negation, a Nihilism. The Not-self doctrine opens

the way to the realization of the *absolute subjectivity* of human consciousness, which the Buddha left unnamed to maintain the expo-
sition of this reality unambiguous: what I point to with Being. Without this apprehension of the Not-self doctrine, the realization of
Buddhism is reduced to a contradiction: a non-existent point of
view, a nihilism.

In one famous sutta, the Buddha points directly to the Nothingness of human consciousness, as that which is beyond the
World of conditioned things:

> *There is, monks, an unborn — unbecome — unmade — unfabricated.*
> *If there were not that unborn — unbecome — unmade — unfabricated,*
> *there would not be the case that emancipation from the born — become*
> *— made — fabricated would be discerned. But precisely because there*
> *is an unborn — unbecome — unmade — unfabricated, that emanci-*
> *pation from the born — become — made — fabricated is discerned.*

(Ud 8.3) (Nibbana 2013)

In other words, human consciousness must originate outside the
world of conditioned things, must be unconditioned, in order to
have awareness of conditioned things, and to be capable of procur-
ing emancipation.

Once essential Being is realized—Enlightenment—then we can
proceed to methodically cleanse the mind of all the bad habits we
have accumulated in our life as Self. Any entity, then, which arises
in the field of consciousness is something which we have created
out of our contact with the world, is an impermanent condition,
and is not Being. Ideas, beliefs, emotions, perceptions, and all I
have created in my interaction with the world, all I can appreciate
to come and go without my grasping them. As I do this more and
more, I become more and more centered in Being, in my experience of existing.

What the Buddha called the Unbinding (Nibbana, in the Pali
language, or Nirvana in Sanskrit), is that consciousness which has
accomplished a complete emancipation from the World as Self: it

is totally at peace and unmoved from its center in Being; here, there is a complete liberation from identification with a Self; here, there is total Freedom of mind and Authentic Happiness; here, the glass of water has been emptied.

Human conscious existence is already a nihilation of the World; which means that it is in essence, or naturally, Not-self: what some Buddhist schools refer to as Original Mind. It is with this understanding that the Mahayana Buddhist insist that everyone is already a Buddha. Indeed, we come to self-consciousness through a nihilation of the World. It is this nihilation which allows us to apprehend the existence of the world, and it is the world which allows us to discern our own existence. Without the world, as Sartre says, we exist all at once: like a floodlight aimed out into pure darkness, the light is undetected even though it does not cease to exist. We become individuals through our being in time and existing as a Self; albeit in this process we become entangled with the World.

We suffer because we are ignorant of the nature of our physical existence, ignorant of the nature of suffering, and ignorant of how we hurt ourselves when we intend to hurt others: this is our contingency of saltwater.

We suffer because we are not of the world, because as a nihilation of the world, we are left alien to it. We suffer because this Self which we embrace is a false Self we hold in Bad Faith. Our Nothingness constantly haunts our existence in the world, as no-thing can ever full-fill that emptiness; we are condemned to a life of lacking and exigencies, like Sisyphus absurdly rolling the rock up the hill, never finding rest. Yet, it is this Nothingness, this emptiness, which also motivates our search for true happiness, for autonomy, for true Freedom.

Enlightenment is the beginning of our journey towards the emancipation of Being, towards Unbinding. Once we have that fundamental insight into the nature of our consciousness as not anything of the World, we can nurture it with ongoing mindfulness of everything we do in our daily routines. As the World becomes more Not-self, as we become increasingly accustomed to not grasping the World, our Being becomes increasingly discernible and unaffected.

This Being has also been called the Ordinary Mind, but there is nothing ordinary about it. Our consciousness of existence only seems ordinary because it is our everyday thing. But once we realize the true nature of the World as Not-self, then the extraordinary nature of our Being becomes evident. What I apprehend in my meditations, when all thoughts and all perceptions disappear, is that I am who gives everything in the world its existence, its sense of reality, its being there: Consciousness is not receptive of the World, but creative! A rose, for example, is exactly nothing in and of itself, it is I who makes its red petals, its green leaves, and its thorns real; it is I who makes it beautiful, poetic, and a symbol of love: it is I who calls it into being. It is in this sense that Being is what is most obvious, most abstruse, and most profound.

To think, to read, to remember, to observe, to move the body, all require attention and mental effort, but to be conscious is spontaneous, requires no effort on our part. When the body and mind are exhausted from intense activity, awareness is not decreased—you are not less conscious—you are just aware of being spent. To exist as Being, to be, is effortless. When we learn to live unattached of the World, then there is nothing that is necessary, nothing to accomplish, nothing to become: Being is just to be.

Being is not any-thing, and it is everything. It is the awareness of our own existence in the act of existing, and of everything else in the world as existing. Being is the miracle of human consciousness.

I was observing children at play in the sun one afternoon. Some were chasing each other laughing, some arguing and pushing each other, others walking holding hands, others peacefully playing games; but all oblivious to the concerns of daily life, to the absurd-ity of death, to the unfathomable complexities and precisions which sustain each moment of life and each second of the universe, for them to play in the sun. Most of us grow old as children: fighting, loving, dancing, crying, and dying, with little awareness of the profound mystery which is our existence: unaware of just how wonderful life could be without a care for the World, abiding in the peacefulness and happiness of just Being with each other.

Bibliography

The Amaravati Sangha. 2013. "Karaniya Metta Sutta: The Buddha's Words on Loving-Kindness" (Sn 1.8), translated from the Pali by The Amaravati Sangha. *Access to Insight (Legacy Edition)*, 2 November 2013. Accessed November 3, 2018. http://www.accesstoinsight.org/tipitaka/kn/snp/snp.1.08.amar.html .

Biro, David. 2010. "Is There Such a Thing as Psychological Pain? and Why It Matters." Accessed November 3, 2018. https://www.ncbi.nlm.nih.gov/pmc/articles/PMC2952112/

Jaspers, Karl. 1951. *Way to Wisdom*. New Haven: Yale University Press.

MIT Technology Review. 2009. "New Measure of Human Brain Processing Speed." Accessed November 3, 2018. https://www.technologyreview.com/s/415041/new-measure-of-human-brain-processing-speed/

"Nibbana: *nibbana*", edited by Access to Insight. *Access to Insight (BCBS Edition)*, 30 November 2013, http://www.accesstoinsight.org/ptf/dhamma/sacca/sacca3/nibbana.html

Seligman Ph.D., Martin E.P. 2002. *Authentic Happiness: Using the New Positive Psychology to Realize Your Potential for Lasting Fulfillment*. New York: The Free Press, a Division of Simon and Schuster.

University of Pennsylvania School of Medicine. 2006. "Penn Researchers Calculate How Much the Retina Tells the Brain." Accessed November 3, 2018. https://www.eurekalert.org/pub_releases/2006-07/uops-prc072606.php

Whitman, Walt. 2004. The Portable Walt Whitman. New York: Penguin Books.

Made in the USA
Coppell, TX
01 November 2020

40629079R00097